What Health Care Professionals Say About *Babywise II*

As an Asia- and America-trained pediatrician, I know the principles of *Babywise II* work cross-culturally. Here is a resource that will help parents guide their babies with confidence and success through the three major transitions of the first year, feeding time, waketime and sleeptime. From experience with my two sons, daughter and countless number of patients, I can enthusiastically recommend all the *Babywise* books as a must-read for competent parenting.

Saphry-May Liauw, M.D., M.S. (Pharm)
Jakarta, Indonesia

As a practicing pediatric neurologist, husband, and father, I fully endorse and highly recommend *Babywise II*. The principles found in this book are immensely practical and universally applicable. If the principles of structure and routine found in this resource were widely applied in the early months and years as they should be, I would see far fewer patients over the age of two with behavioral deficiencies and neurologic challenges. Virtually all of the books available on child development, behavior management and attention disorders fall far short when compared to the wisdom, practicality, and confidence offered in this one resource.

Robert P. Turner, M.D.
Richmond, Virginia

As a *Babywise* pediatrician, every newborn baby is a challenge and excitement to me, because I know I can help them with their moral behaviors as well as their physical well-being. *Babywise II* enables me to contribute to the structure and behavior of children, which is much needed in our society. This wonderful, practical, effective my practice, since no other medical textbook strikes so deeply into the basic needs of life.

Peter Y. S. Kim, M.D.
Valencia, California

Finally, a parenting guide that is practical, makes sense and works! *Babywise II* provides today's parents with the up-to-date parenting strategies needed for a new millennium. As a pediatric professional, I enthusiastically recommend this book as a vital road map for the pre-toddler months.

Penn Laird, M.D.
Pediatric Cardiologist
Dallas, Texas

ON BECOMING

BABY WISE

BOOK TWO

Parenting Your Five to Twelve Month Old
Through the Babyhood Transitions

GARY EZZO, M.A. AND
ROBERT BUCKNAM, M.D.

PARENT-WISE SOLUTIONS, INC.

ON BECOMING BABYWISE BOOK II
Understanding the Babyhood Transitions
(Parenting Your Five to Twelve Month Old)

4th Edition

® "ON BECOMING" is a registered trademark

ISBN: 978-0-9714532-1-0

Printed in the United States of America

Parent-Wise Solutions
(Administration and Inquiries)
2160 Cheswick Lane
Mount Pleasant, SC 29466

www.parentwisesolutions.com

11 12 13 14 — 36 35 34 33

Dedicated To:
Robyn and Gary Vander Weide

Two points of light shining bright,
two friends walking close

ACKNOWLEDGMENTS

We are grateful for the assistance of many co-workers from the past and the present including: Tim and Patricia Lentz, Scott and Theresa McLeod, David and Cynthia Iglesias, Tiana Wendelburg, Sharon Augustson. They were all instrumental in the success of this book. We would also like to thank Connie Lamoureux who contributed the narrative on language development (Appendix A), and Nancy Martin and sketch artist, Yvonne Wilber for their contribution on sign-language training. We are grateful for Paige Hunter and Carla Link's recent editorial contributions, which we highly prize and greatly appreciate.

We have a valuable resource in Dr. Alan Furness, another friend who provided recommendations for proper dental care of infants and toddlers. Finally, we wish to acknowledge Sarah Blunk for her assistance relating to the Mozart Effect discussed in Chapter Six. What makes this acknowledgement special is we have known Sarah from childhood and watched her grow into adulthood as a beautiful young woman, inside and out.

CONTENTS

Forward

As a pediatrician, the healthy growth of children is the central concern of my practice. By definition, "healthy" means more than just positive ear, nose, and throat examinations. Healthy growth includes physical, moral, and academic fitness. It includes giving your baby what is best while avoiding those things that can hurt or delay him. As is the case with all aspects of child training, good parenting begins with Mom and Dad and what they consider to be their priorities in child training.

For example, parenting arouses many different emotions throughout the day and week—for parent and baby. Love, joy, peace, contentment, and confidence are easily matched by the emotions of frustration, disappointment, discouragement, and on some days, despair when things just don't go according to the book.

Parenting to achieve all the right emotions however, is not the priority goal of child-training—yet many parents act on that belief. For these, childrearing is reduced to avoidance of all negative emotions and pursuit of positive ones. Right and wrong training is then measured by how parents think their child feels, rather than by the end product—what is best for the child. If the child feels happy, the parent is satisfied. If the child feels sad, then the parent works to create an environment that will eliminate his or her sadness regardless of the context of that sadness. That approach is not healthy for children, families, or society in general.

One of the greatest acts of benevolence within the home takes place when parents provide their children the gift of *self-control*. Self-control is a base virtue leading to healthy and productive self-management of life, and the foundations for this potential reality are laid very early in the parenting process. In fact, if you're a *Babywise* parent you probably already laid this foundation with the employment of a basic feed, wake and naptime routine.

Children who have internal self-control and mastery of the "please and thank you's" of life also have the self-control that will help them secure a healthy academic and relational life. The self-control that keeps a child sitting in a highchair without fighting with mom is the same self-control that will later keep him at a desk with a book in his hand. *Babywise* laid down the right foundation; *Babywise II* provides the right structure for creating a suitable learning environment for advancing any child in the crucial disciplines of life.

Yet, this book offers so much more than a sure pathway leading to future self-control. *Babywise II* is also about the subtle transitions in the three activities of your baby's day: feeding times, waketimes and naptimes. Everything is changing and the more you grow in your understanding of these babyhood transitions, the more confident you will become in managing your baby's world. *Babywise II* is here to help. Thank you for joining us in this next step in the journey in parenting.

Robert Bucknam, M.D.

Introduction

I t's reality-check time! You're at least four months into your tour of parenting and the complexity of child-training is starting to multiply. As your baby grows physically, so does his mind; adapting with an ever-increasing awareness of new sensations, sights, sounds and relationships. Now that your baby is interacting with his material universe with greater attentiveness, big changes are coming. How should Mom and Dad approach the various growth transitions? Certainly not by abandoning that which brought them so much initial success—their baby's routine. No, they will want to preserve the order and structure that brought security to their baby's day, peaceful sleep to their baby's nights, and stability to their home. While the principles that brought the initial success will not change, the application of those principles must adapt in light of their babies exponential growth over the next six months.

In truth, by the mid-year mark, babies begin intentionally interacting with the various nouns that make up his developing world; i.e., people, places and things. This is when life for baby and Mom moves from the wonderfully simple to challenging and complex. For example, feeding time is more than a biological response dictated by a baby's sucking reflex. For the six-month old, mealtime becomes a very complex and conscious interaction between child and parent, food and drink, preference and need, likes and dislikes, must do and won't do!

Waketime behaviors begin to fall into the categories off 'right' and 'wrong' and will either be encouraged or discouraged by how Mom and Dad respond to the many new ways their baby expresses his curiosity. In fact, right and wrong patterns of behavior are a part of a baby's entire day. This is why feeding time, waketime, and bedtime will provide numerous opportunities to display parental wisdom, guidance and certainly patience; all enshrined by a growing understanding of what a parent can expect during the *Babywise II* months.

A word about this revised and updated edition: it really does take talent to explain the neuroscience of a baby's brain and how parents can profoundly influence advanced forms of learning in children and what things they do to hinder or disrupt learning structures. The many references to the developing brain of infants and toddlers comes from the assistance of long-time friend and medical consultant, Dr. Robert Turner. As a pediatric neurologist, Dr. Turner's gift of time and attention to the growing body of research and breakthroughs in neuroscience will benefit our readers for generations to come.

The practical nature of *Babywise II* allows parents to take advantage of the information provided. But those best served are the graduates of our first book, *Babywise*. In *Babywise*, we introduced the foundational principles this book continues to build on, including routine feedings, naps, and the establishment of healthy nighttime sleep. Those not familiar with the concepts of *Babywise* should become acquainted with the guiding principles in that book first before moving forward with *Babywise II*.

In addition, the reader will find two important appendices in the back of this manual: Appendix A: "Your Child's Language Development"; and Appendix B: "What Makes Your Baby a Person", a summary explaining the controlling influences that go into making your baby a person. Please read them at your convenience.

Finally, as was the case with *Babywise*, we can give you trustworthy ideas and workable solutions, but not every possible application. As you read through each chapter, it's vital that you think in terms of *principle*. Understanding a 'principle' of parenting, derived from your own beliefs and values, is a greater asset than just having a list of 'how-to' answers. Principle parenting is an extension of wisdom parenting.

We know many rewarding experiences are just around the corner as you move into this next exciting phase of parenting.

Gary Ezzo

Section One

Mealtime Transitions

Chapter One
Begin as You Mean to Go

❧

Throughout a baby's first year, two processes continue to dominate: growth and learning. These activities are interdependent, but not interchangeable. *Growth* refers to the biological processes of life; *learning* refers to the mental processes, which include moral training and development. With both growth and learning, the building blocks are progressive. Each stage of development depends on the successful completion of the previous stage.

FACTORS OF GROWTH

Every species, whether animal or human, follows a pattern of development peculiar to that species. With children, there is evidence of natural orderly rule in postnatal development. Infants demonstrate two growth patterns: vertically from the head down to the feet and horizontally from the central axis of the body toward the extremities.

Descending vertical development means strength in physical structure and function come first to the child's head region, then to the child's trunk, and last to his legs and feet. Your baby first started to lift his head, bob it a little, and then let it fall back to the mattress. Next, he could hold his head upright as a result of his developing neck and chest muscles. At the age of twenty weeks, he had control over the muscles of his eyes, head, and shoulders, but his trunk was still so limp that he had to be propped up or strapped in a chair to be able to maintain a sitting position. He made good use of his arms and hands in reaching and grasping before he could use his legs. Eventually, he motored himself around by creeping, then crawling and then walking, running, jumping, and skipping.

Horizontal development proceeds from simple to complex. In the prenatal state the head and trunk are well-developed before the limbs begin to grow. Gradually, the arms lengthen and then develop into the hands and fingers. Functionally, in the postnatal state, a baby can use his arms before his hands, and can use his hands as a unit before he can control the movements of his fingers. He rakes his food toward his mouth first, before he can master the finer motor skills of the *pincer reflex*. Order is the operative word for biological maturation – physical growth always occurs in an orderly, predictable way.

FACTORS OF LEARNING

Where biological maturation refers to changes in physical capabilities that result from genetic cues, learning signifies changes resulting from interaction with one's environment. For the most part, learning is brought about by parental influence and instruction. Like adults, children interpret new experiences in relationship to knowledge formerly acquired. That means learning is progressive, and a child only gains understanding when new information has meaning in relationship to previous experiences. Routine and orderly transition at each stage of the child's development aid the marriage between new information and a child's understanding. We reinforce this concept with this chapter's refrain: *Begin as you mean to go*.

Why is this important? Because allowing a child to progress in an orderly fashion in his or her new and expanding world greatly enhances learning. It is the gradual assimilation of many perceptions that gives rise to the formation of ideas. The child who can associate right meanings with new experiences is far more advanced in his or her understanding than the child who must associate a new meaning with an old situation that will ultimately need correction.

Since learning comes in progressive stages, child-training should take place in the same way, occurring hand-in-hand with progressions in learning. For this reason, parents need to provide their child with a learning environment that matches information with understanding.

There are many factors that influence learning, both positively and negatively. The child's temperament, the presence or absence of siblings, parental resolve, the purpose for training, the method of instruction, and reinforcement are some of the more obvious ones. Generally speaking, there are three categories of learning: basic skills, academic learning and moral development. Let's take a look at each one.

Basic Skills

Not all behavior is moral in nature. Some actions are morally neutral – such as those related to basic skills. One of the most important and most rapid areas of development during early childhood is the development of motor skills. Learning to drink from a cup, use a spoon, self-feed and walk are all stage acquired activities. They are skills, to a large extent associated with the child's environment, opportunities to learn, and his or her motivation to do so. From the helpless state of infancy, the development of skills begins and moves forward. Most children accomplish these feats in progressive stages. For example, when your baby is first introduced to finger foods, he begins by raking his food with his entire hand and then lifts the food toward his mouth with his fist closed. As his coordination develops, he begins to use just his fingers, then eventually his index finger and thumb, bringing food to his mouth with precision. In a couple of years your toddler will throw a ball using his whole body. As his coordination develops, he will throw the ball using only his arm.

Skills, talents, and giftedness are not the same thing. Skills – such as learning to use a spoon, walk, color within the lines, riding a bike, and throwing a ball – are basic to all human beings. Natural talents differ from skills in that they are discriminatory – some people have a particular talent, others don't. All of us have talents, but not necessarily the same talents. Giftedness is a talent magnified. Many musicians are naturally talented, but Mozart was gifted.

Academic Learning

Academic learning is the accumulation of data and the ability to apply logic (reasoning skills) to a given situation. Academic learning, much like physical development, moves from general to specific and is progressive. We teach our children the alphabet so they can learn to put letters together to form words, then eventually read those words. They first learn to count 1, 2, 3, 4, 5 but it will be a while before they realize that those same numbers can also represent $12,345. Children first learn about trees in general, then begin to distinguish, for example, a pine tree from an oak tree. Eventually, they will learn to identify the different varieties of pine trees. However, the connections in the brain that makes all of this understandable to a child is not formed randomly but through activity and purposeful training. Please keep this in mind!

Moral Development

At birth, a child has no functioning conscience. Young children do not have the moral means to create or respond to right and wrong. This does not mean, however, that you suspend the training of right responses. For example, the fact that a child has no moral understanding of why food shouldn't be intentionally dropped from his or her highchair doesn't mean parents should hold back instruction or correction for this situation.

With adults, beliefs precede actions, but with pretoddlers and toddlers, the opposite is true – actions precede beliefs. This is why parents should insist on right responses long before their children are capable of understanding moral concepts. Young children first learn how to act appropriately then they learn how to think morally. Just because a six-month-old is not capable of moral distinction in the way he behaves, does not mean basic foundations are not being laid. They are!

The first step toward reasoning skills and comprehension is the development of healthy learning patterns. Structure and your baby's basic routine enhance these patterns and the neuro-pathways in your baby's brain welcome them. When a child is at peace with his basic environment, his learning potential increases and learning disorders are minimized. Routine and order facilitates this positive conclusion.

Routine and orderly advancement encourages *self-control*. Self-control is a foundational virtue, meaning other virtues are dependent on it. Self-control influences kindness, gentleness, proper speech, controlling negative emotions, concentrating, focusing, sitting skills and many other behaviors. When you train your child to a right response, (yes, even in the highchair), you are simultaneously training him in self-control. It is a gift every parent can and should give their child.

21

Chapter Two
Introducing Solid Foods

I n *Babywise,* we introduced the three activities of a baby's day – feeding time, waketime, and naptime. With age-appropriate modifications these activities continue to serve as your guide for the next six months. Each activity has it's own benefits and challenges as your baby approaches his or her sixth month birthday. This segment addresses the adjustments you make as your baby moves into the next feeding transition; the introduction of solid foods. Where do you begin?

PRAYER
We believe life is more than a cosmic accident that happened without rhyme or reason. The existence of a personal, benevolent, orderly God is part of our world view. If this is part of your belief, you might consider introducing a prayer of thanks at each mealtime. Parents act as substitutes for their children in several different ways. For example, we are to serve as their moral conscience until their own hearts are fully operative. We also make wise decisions on their behalf until they grow in wisdom. And we offer heavenly thanks on their behalf for the food they receive. The first eternal truth your child will participate in is touching the throne of God with prayer. When you pray with your child, hold his or her little hands and say, "Let's bow our heads and thank God." What a joy it is to have a fifteen-month-old who voluntarily waits before he or she eats

until a prayer of thanks is offered.

SIGNS OF READINESS

The introduction of solid foods does not mean the suspension of liquid feedings. The calories gained from breastmilk or formula are still of prime importance. However, your baby is reaching a growth point where neither solid foods nor liquid feedings are nutritionally sufficient alone. Both are required. The amount needed from each food source will be discussed later in this visit.

As a general rule, babies usually start solid food between the ages of four and six months. Although the American Academy of Pediatrics leans more toward six months, your baby's pediatrician will direct you based on your child's unique nutritional needs.

There are some developmental signs to look for before offering solids. We support the common opinion that solid foods should only be introduced after your child is able to control his neck and head muscles and sit with support. This usually aligns with the baby who can lift his head off a blanket and sustain the position. Prior to this achievement, your baby should only receive his daily nourishment through breastmilk or formula.

There are other indicators of readiness. Your baby might be ready for solids if he shows signs of hunger even though he is receiving 32 oz. of formula a day. The breastfeeding equivalent would be your baby showing signs of hunger after six to eight full breastfeeds in a twenty-four hour period. For the baby who has a well-established nighttime sleep pattern, any abnormal waking at night between five and six months of age, or waking early during naps, might also signal that more nutrition is required during the day.

The Five Food Stages

Feeding becomes increasingly complex as your baby grows. For that reason baby food manufactures often categorize each food transition into stages. Each stage represents another level of food mixture and nutritional complexity. They are presented here as age-related guides and suggestions. By no means should they be viewed as absolute rules or requirements for feeding your baby. However, since we will be referring to these stages throughout your reading, we desire that you become familiar with each one.

Stage One: (4 to 6 months) Single-grain cereal and single ingredient baby foods.

Stage Two: (6 to 7 months) Single ingredient and combination foods; vegetables and fruits for added variety and flavor.

Stage Three: (8 to 12 months) A new range of textures, slightly coarser than strained foods, packaged in larger containers for growing appetites. (At this age the AAP recommends a baby receive between 750 to 900 calories each day with 400 to 500 coming from breastmilk or formula.)

Stage Four: (12 to 15 months) Regular family meals supplemented with some baby food.

Stage Five: (15 months and up) Prepared regular family meals, no baby food supplement necessary.

Mastering a New Skill

One would think that eating comes as naturally as breathing.

Not so for infants. Introducing solids requires a new skill level from your baby and a series of new responses. Initially your baby may tongue thrust his cereal out of his mouth. In fact, expect to see this. This is not a sign that he doesn't like his food, but rather that he doesn't know what to do with it. Swallowing solids off a foreign object (the spoon) is much different than swallowing milk. The good news is that these challenges are short-lived and your baby will quickly learn how to take food from a spoon.

If you experience a strong resistance from your baby toward a particular food, consider suspending its introduction for a few weeks then try again. Some researchers suggest it may take a dozen attempts before the child willingly accepts your food selection. The benefit that eventually comes from your persistence is that your soon-to-be toddler is less likely to be a picky eater and more likely to be a willing participant with your family's normal food menu.

Check for Allergic Reactions

One basic rule of introducing solids is to begin with one item at time, waiting three to five days to see if your baby develops an allergic reaction. Sequential introduction of food items allows you to monitor your baby's reaction so proper nutritional adjustments can be made if needed. For example, your baby might do fine with yellow squash, but have an intestinal reaction to peas. Rashes and diarrhea are common symptoms of food allergies in babies. Vomiting, while rare, is a more serious indicator. The bottom line? Never introduce multiple food sources at the same time. If you do, you will not know which food caused the reaction.

GETTING STARTED WITH RICE CEREAL

Mothers are naturally concerned about the nutritional health of their babies, and they should be. Infants have unique nutritional needs that must be met to promote healthy growth. By their mid-year mark, most breastfed babies need nutrients beyond those received through breastmilk. Iron and zinc are two of them. Both become essential for your baby's physical growth and brain development. In addition, zinc aids the developing immune system. Infant cereals are a good source of these minerals along with Vitamin C.

Vitamin D is also very important. Babies need this specific vitamin to help them grow strong bones and teeth. Babies who do not get enough Vitamin D are at risk for rickets, a disease that affects the way bones grow. While breastmilk is the perfect food for your baby, Vitamin D supplements are usually required for breastfeeding mothers, especially after five months. If your baby is receiving formula, he is getting the necessary daily requirements of Vitamin D and therefore supplements are not usually needed.

There are three cereal food sources that can and should eventually be introduced to your baby's diet. Rice cereal is the most common to begin with because it causes the least amount of allergic reactions. The downside of rice cereal is a potential constipation problem for your baby. You will need to monitor this and alert your pediatrician if the problem persists.

If your pediatrician determines that rice cereal is not the best to start with, oat and barley cereals are two excellent substitutes. We would encourage you to consider eventually introducing all three cereals over the course of a couple of months. Do not introduce wheat cereal without consulting your pediatrician.

When introducing cereal into your baby's diet, start with your most convenient feeding of the day. Remember to be patient with the process. Learning to swallow solids from a spoon is a new skill. As such, the first few feedings tend to be a little messy until your baby gets use to swallowing solids. Taking food from a spoon is usually mastered in three or four days. Some moms prefer to start with a soft rubber tipped spoon as opposed to a metal surface. A bottle-fed infant might possibly show a small preference to plastic, but eventually your baby will adjust to whatever you use.

Do not be overly alarmed if your baby loses interest in eating before you think he should. You will find over the next several months that your baby will not be equally hungry at each meal. If you see him turning his head away from the spoon, thrusting food out of his mouth, or he begins to cry, then mealtime is over. At this point you can return to breastfeeding or offer the rest of his bottle of formula.

How to Begin?

Until your baby is able to sit up by himself, and to minimize the risk of choking, always place him in an upright position, either in your arms or his infant seat while feeding him food. Starting out is as easy as 1, 2, 3, 4.

Day One: Initially, start by mixing one tablespoon of rice cereal with four tablespoons of either breastmilk, formula, or water. (The texture should be similar to a cream of wheat consistency, not overly thick like a paste, nor watery enough to drip off a spoon.) Although you will be making changes to the amount of the cereal/liquid combination, keep the consistency the same. Offer cereal at one meal.

Day Two: Mix 2 tablespoons of rice cereal with your baby's

liquids. Offer at one meal.

<u>Days Three & Four</u>: Increase the mixture to 3 tablespoons on the third day and 4 tablespoons on the fourth day. Maintain consistency by increasing the liquid gradually. Cereal can now be offered twice a day.

<u>Day Five</u>: If there are no allergic reactions by the end of day four, start offering cereal three times a day, using approximately 1/4 cup per meal.

Once you're beyond the first week begin offering your baby solids at the normal feeding times. For example, if you have been breast or bottle-feeding him at 7:00 a.m. (breakfast), 11:00 a.m. (lunch), 3:00 p.m. (dinner), and 7:00 p.m., then solids should accompany at least the three major meals. Over time your baby's feeding times should align with the rest of the family. Since cereal is an excellent source of iron, we suggest you continue at least one serving a day up through the first year.

Regarding the timing of other food sources; you start introducing vegetables approximately two weeks after cereal has been successfully introduced. (See *Introducing Vegetables*)

Combining Breastfeeding and Solids

Breastfeeding mothers should maintain at least four or five nursing periods a day for adequate milk supply. Begin feeding your baby with one breast. Offer solids next, followed by the other breast. If you find that your baby is not taking the solids well, experiment by offering some solids first, then offer the breast, offer solids again, and then finish on the breast. If you are bottle-feeding, offer a quarter to half-a-bottle, then the solid foods, then the remaining amount of formula.

Once you start adding solids to his diet, his daily intake of milk should gradually decrease from 32 ounces a day to about 24 ounces. After your baby is established on all solid foods, he should receive at least 20 ounces of formula per day alongside a varied diet until he is a year old. (Pediatricians normally do not advise moving from formula to cows milk until after baby's first birthday.) Again, if breastfeeding, continue with at least four or five nursing periods a day.

Warning

Experienced moms will tell you not to offer solid foods, then two hours later nurse, followed two hours later with more solids. This is creating a "snacker" and will disrupt your child's hunger and sleep-wake stabilization. Even at mealtime, stay mindful of training so as to avoid retraining. Guard against allowing poor eating habits to take root, such as snacking between meals, fingers in the mouth, playing with food, and spitting food out. In parenting, it will always be easier to train your child in the way he should go rather than retraining sometime later when behaviors are out of control.

INTRODUCING VEGETABLES

Once your baby starts to receive three cereal portions a day, he's ready for vegetables. Start with the noon meal, introducing yellow vegetables (squash or carrots) first. Watch for any allergic reaction. Three or four days later introduce a green vegetable (peas or beans). Over time, expand the choices of primary vegetables matching those most familiar to your family. Although vegetables are being added to your baby's diet, continue to supplement each meal with a liquid feeding.

Serving Portions

Make it a habit to read the labels on the baby-food jars and cereal boxes. Understand the list of ingredients, storage recommendations and serving instructions provided by the manufacturer. Normally, baby-food jars used in Stage One, contain 2 1/2 ounces of food. Containers used in Stage Two hold 3 1/2 ounces.

Each time you introduce another food group (vegetables, fruits or meats), start with half a jar or less for a few days, watching for excessive fussiness, rashes, runny nose, diarrhea, or watery eyes, all of which are possible signs of food allergies. By day four or five, increase the vegetables to one small jar twice a day, usually at lunch and dinner. And please think long term. Over time, gradually offer your baby a variety of food tastes. This will help decrease the possibility of a picky or finicky eater down the road. This is a good place to remind you to *begin as you mean to go.*

At Stage Two (6-7 months), move to the larger baby-food jars and serve approximately 3 ounces at least twice a day (one jar at lunch and one at dinner). You can continue this through the eighth month and until you begin offering home-prepared vegetables.

We offer one word of caution here: beware of too many yellow vegetables (i.e. squash and carrots). Some babies enjoy squash and carrots so much it becomes the serving food of choice for Mom. But too many yellow vegetables in your baby's diet can cause his skin tone to turn slightly orange. This is not a sign of jaundice but rather a harmless condition known as *carotenemia* due to the carotene contained in the yellow vegetables. If you see this happening, vary your baby's diet by reducing the amount of yellow vegetables.

INTRODUCING FRUITS

Because your baby needs the nutrition that comes from vegetables, fruits should be used as a complementary food source to vegetables but not a substitute for them. Fruits are naturally sweet, so children will prefer them over their cereal and vegetables. Therefore, offer vegetables first and cereal or fruit-flavored cereal last.

How Much Fruit at Each Serving?
5 to 6 months - 1 1/2 to 2 oz. twice a day
7 months - 3 to 4 oz. twice a day
8 months - 4 to 6 oz. twice a day
9-12 months - Introduce soft, mashed or cut-up fruits (bananas, applesauce, avocados, pears, peaches, prunes, or berries with no seeds.)

As a reminder, pay attention to the listed age-recommended amounts on the baby-food jars. If you have any questions, check with your pediatrician's office for their suggested guidelines and recommendations. Like vegetables, not all fruits can be introduced to your baby. Before ten months, do not offer your baby whole grapes, cherry tomatoes, or citrus fruits. These items can be mashed into servings but never given whole. Eventually your baby's menu will look similar to this:

Breakfast: Cereal and fruits
Lunch: Vegetables and fruits
Dinner: Cereal, vegetables, and fruits

INTRODUCING MEATS

Babies need protein to build muscles and to strengthen their immune systems. Because breastmilk and formula are excellent sources of highly digestible protein, meats are not necessary to meet your baby's protein needs. Therefore, you should hold off giving your baby meats until he is fully established on vegetables and fruits. Health-wise, meats can be held off until Stage Three (8-12 months), and 2 1/2 ounces a day will be sufficient to meet your baby's nutritional needs. We recommend you offer a meat selection at the mid-day meal.

As with the other food sources, offer a single meat at a time and watch for an allergic response. Avoid processed meats because they tend to have high sodium content. You can introduce a cooked egg yolk after meats have been accepted. Egg whites are linked to food reactions and should not be introduced until after a baby's first birthday. Like all foods, you will want to be nutritionally wise when it comes to meats. Read all the labels and understand what types of meats you're offering.

THE CHALLENGE OF CHOICE

Feeding your baby supplemental foods is probably easier than sorting through all the potential available choices. If the modern mom only had to deal with cereal, vegetables and fruits, the task would be fairly straightforward. One challenge parents are facing today is the varieties of mixed-food sources offered by baby food manufacturers. It is not just a cereal option, but cereals mixed with fruits, or cereals mixed with vegetables, or vegetables mixed with fruits. Multiply the number of vegetables with the number of fruits and the final figure will explain why the baby food section takes up half-an-aisle at the neighborhood grocers.

Does you baby really need all those varieties? Probably not. Just keep in mind that your little one has no food or flavor expectations until you create them. Our recommendation is to keep each food group separate until all have been introduced routinely. After that, feel free to explore the cereal/fruit or fruit/vegetable combinations. Just realize that once you sweeten the cereal or vegetables, it may be more difficult to offer individual items later because your pretoddler can and will develop preferences.

MAKING YOUR OWN BABY FOOD

Preparing your own baby food is an easy, money-saving alternative to store-bought brands. If home preparation is your choice, be sure you only use organic foods as they contain no nitrites derived from soil fertilizers. Nitrites have been linked to a type of anemia in babies. Safe food sources make for healthy babies.

It is easy to prepare vegetables such as carrots, peas, green beans, yams, sweet potatoes, and butternut squash (and they freeze well). To prepare carrots, peas, or green beans, boil in water until tender. Puree in a blender, adding small amounts of purified water as needed. To prepare yams, sweet potatoes, or squash, cook them in the oven until very soft. Remove the skin and any seeds, then puree the remainder in a blender with purified water.

When preparing large quantities for freezing, always sterilize your containers. When needed, thaw the food in your refrigerator. Cookbooks are a good resource for baby food preparation, and much safer than internet resources. Books have to be screened and edited before being published and printed. Anyone can post their ideas, good or bad, on the internet without accountability. Please be careful what advice you find on the internet.

JUICES

Fruit juices are not only the last of the food options to become part of your baby's diet, but the least necessary. While you can introduce juices as early as six months, we recommend holding off until Stage Three (8-12 months). Juices are more of a "fun alternative" for your baby than an necessary nutrient source. A better nutritional option to juices are fresh fruits run through a food processor or blender. Apples, pears, kiwi and grapes blended to a 'sauce' texture are a refreshing and healthy treat. (Avoid pulp-filled citrus fruits and juices until after your baby's first year. Pulp is difficult for a baby to swallow and could cause choking.)

Store-bought juice drinks come with some strict government labeling facts. The U.S. Food and Drug Administration wants consumers to know that there is a difference between fruit juices and fruit drinks. Fruit juices are labeled 100% fruit juice with no additives. Fruit drinks only have a percentage of fruit juice, supplemented with added sugars and sulfates. Your baby should not have any fruit drinks until he is well into the toddler years and pasteurized juices are the safest.

It is because juices are naturally sweet that they can and should be diluted 50% - 60% with water. They do not have to be offered everyday. Begin with 3 to 4 ounces of apple, grape or cranberry, once a day and over the next four months gradually increase to 6 ounces a day. We suggest you limit the juices to mealtimes, offering them in a sippy cup, not a bottle. In fact, avoid offering juices from the bottle altogether. This includes putting a child down for a nap with a bottle of juice. In a reclining position, the juice sugars can easily collect leading to tooth decay. When your baby moves into the toddler years, diluted juices make a good afternoon snack.

INTRODUCING THE SIPPY CUP

Parents can begin to introduce the sippy cup around five to six months. By no means is the cup a substitute for the bottle or Mom, but it is a new skill that your baby will soon master. Breastmilk, formula or water are great starting liquids while juices will come much later.

Like baby bottles, sippy cups come in an assortment of colors, shapes, sizes and styles. Some come with handles, others with replacement spouts. The most important aspect of any cup is the "no drip, no spill" feature. As far as the child is concerned, it should be one that is easy to hold and allows the liquid to flow freely.

When first introducing the sippy cup, it would be wise to have a bib or cloth handy. Since your baby is not used to receiving liquid in this manner, much of what goes in the mouth will come out. Get cleaver with the preventative side of this training. For example, some moms start introducing the sipping cup during their baby's bath so cleaning up is fairly easy.

There are benefits to introducing the sippy cup early. One is convenience because nothing has to be prepared. Fill the cup with water and take it on any outing for a quick drink. You can also offer it after he wakes from his afternoon nap or when out shopping with Mom. By introducing the sippy cup early, weaning your baby becomes a much smoother transition. Weaning from the bottle is covered at the end of the next section.

However you achieve your success the word to remember is *perseverance*. Your baby will catch on to drinking from a cup very quickly, but you have to stay consistent in those early days of training. In a matter of a few months, he will be holding his own cup, taking drinks at will and even asking you for more while signing "please" and "thank you". And when you begin to see that happen, you will realize how wonderfully amazing your child's mind really is. He is ready to learn! Are you ready to lead and teach?

Chapter Three
Finger Foods & Snacks

Your child's readiness for highchair finger foods signals another marvelous advancement in his development – hand-finger-mouth coordination. This too is another food transition, moving baby from total dependence on Mom or Dad to self-feeding.

The ability to self-feed starts with your child's *raking* and *pincer reflex*. The raking reflex develops between seven and eight months. This is when a baby begins to rake his highchair finger foods toward him with his entire hand and then grasps with all fingers. It is the whole hand that goes to the mouth, not simply the fingers. The pincer reflex is an advanced skill of infancy, usually acquired around nine months. Your baby now has the ability to pinch items between his thumb and forefinger. The item is brought to the mouth with his fingers alone.

Finger foods should be kept safe and simple. The items should be soft enough to break into small pieces and swallowed easily. Small pieces of cut-up banana, cereal such as Cheerios[tm], puffed rice or wafer-type crackers are good finger foods. Eventually you will add well-cooked peas or green beans cut in small pieces and small bites of potato. Baby food manufacturers also offer a variety of nutritious and safe assortments for Stage Three and Four finger foods. Your pediatrician can provide a recommended list of age-appropriate foods.

Although your baby may have a few teeth, it is very important that the texture of finger foods be very soft so that your baby can "gum" the foods. This might require that you steam the item to the appropriate softness. If you question whether a particular food item is safe for your baby, put it in your mouth. Does it dissolve, melt, or break up into small pieces? If it doesn't, do not offer it before one year of age.

As your child approaches his first birthday, finger food selections will expand. Steamed vegetables like carrots and peas, well-cooked pasta, or scramble eggs will become food options. (Most pediatricians suggest a baby not receive the white of the egg prior to one year of age.)

There is a 'never do' list for finger foods. Never offer a baby a spoonful of peanut butter or nuts in general, uncooked peas, celery, raw carrots, whole cherry tomatoes, whole grapes, or any hard, round food. Always check with your pediatrician for his or her recommended finger food list.

One final note relating to solid foods: As your baby's diet changes, his stools will change color and consistency, becoming more firm. If the opposite happens (loose or watery stools or stools filled with mucus), it is usually a sign that the digestive track is irritated. This condition should be brought immediately to the attention of your baby's pediatrician. However, a drastic change in stool color does not necessarily indicate a problem, but is usually associated with the type of food your baby is receiving. Beets will turn stools red and peas will turn them green. These color changes are fairly predictable and considered normal. Unfortunately, for those doing diaper changes, the strong, unpleasant odor of digested foods will become commonplace for the next two years, until toilet training is accomplished.

Snacks

Snacks are a fun treat for your Stage Four and Five child (12 to 15 months of age). But like all things, a balanced approach is needed. Snacks should not become a substitute meal. Offering too many at the wrong times only encourages poor eating habits and sets the stage for a picky eater. If you see that happening, cut back on the amount of snacks offered or cut them out altogether. Here are a few helpful hints about snacking:

1. You don't have to offer a snack everyday.
2. Moderation is key. Do not let snacks detract from a hearty appetite.
3. Do not use food to avoid conflict.
4. As your child stays awake longer, avoid using food as a pacifier.
5. The place for snacking should be consistent, such as a Bumbo Baby Seat or highchair. Avoid allowing your child to crawl or walk around the house or store with a juice drink or snack in his hand.
6. As a general suggestion, offer snacks in the afternoon, such as after your child wakes from his nap.

THE FINICKY EATER

Like all people, your baby will show preferences in taste. While you will occasionally give your pretoddler what he likes, you must also consider what meets the nutritional needs and desires of the entire family. When age-appropriate, offer foods that your family normally eats. This should be a natural food transition for your baby. Sometimes you might have to persevere with some choices but in time your baby will begin to enjoy the foods you enjoy.

When it comes to food and fussiness, finicky eaters are often

41

created by parental fears and dislikes rather than any genetic predisposition on the child's part. As a parent, you might have to evaluate your own relationship with food. Are you overly concerned with nutritional intake, a picky eater yourself, or a junk-food connoisseur? As hard as it may be, try not to pass on any overly anxious preoccupation with food or poor nutritional habits to your children.

Just as it is when introducing solids, if you experience any strong resistance toward a particular taste or texture, stop and wait a few weeks, then try again. Young pretoddlers usually acquire a taste for the foods they previously rejected. Persistence does pay off and your baby will be less likely to become a picky/finicky eater as a result.

Finally, try to make mealtime a pleasant experience for all. Some of the most pleasant memories of life for children come from the times shared around the dinner table as a family. While we place books, computers, plants and newspapers on our kitchen table, the most important use comes when family members congregate around it at mealtime. Here are some age-appropriate suggestions to make mealtime a joyful family time.

For children under six months: When possible, place your baby in his infant seat near the dinner table. Being able to see and hear the family interacting is important to the establishment of early family identity. When it is just Mom or Dad, get into the habit of talking with your baby during mealtime. While there might be some occasions when mealtime for the rest of the family will be playpen time for the baby, this will be limited.

Six to twelve months (or until the child can feed himself): At this age, your baby may actually eat his main meal before the rest of the family sits down. Then, while the family enjoys their meal together, the baby can sit in his highchair with a toy or some finger foods if he is older. Now everyone is participating, and Mom can enjoy her meal as well.

Twelve months and older: Family mealtime should be characterized by everyone eating together. To keep the evening meal pleasant, put more concentrated effort into highchair problems at breakfast and lunch. This does not mean you will not correct during dinner, however, the concentrated effort at the other meals can speed up the process of dining harmony.

WEANING YOUR BABY

Weaning, by today's definition, is the process by which parents offer food supplements in place of, or in addition to, mother's milk. This process begins the moment you give your baby formula or when he first tastes cereal. From that moment on, weaning is a gradual process.

From the Breast

The duration of breastfeeding varies depending on Mom and baby's mutual desires and needs. While there are many opinions, no one can say for sure what age is ideal for your unique situation. For some it may be six months, for others a year or more. (A year is a very achievable goal.) Breastfeeding for more than a year is a matter of preference since adequate supplementary food is usually available. During biblical times, weaning took place between eighteen and twenty-four months; three years was more the exception than the rule.

At birth, infants depend totally on their caregiver to meet

their physical needs, but they gradually become more independent by taking "baby steps". One such step for your baby is the ability to feed himself. You can begin by eliminating one nursing period at a time, waiting three to four days before dropping the next feeding. This time-frame allows the mother's body to make the proper adjustment in her milk production.

The late-afternoon feeding is usually the easiest to drop since it is a busy time of day. Replace each feeding with six to eight ounces of formula or milk (depending on the child's age). Pediatricians generally recommend that parents not give their baby cow's milk until they are at least one year old. If your baby is nine months or older, consider going straight to a sippy cup rather than to a bottle. This transition will be easiest if you have introduced the cup prior to weaning.

Stay mindful that once your baby moves into the toddler phase, he requires at least one-thousand calories a day for normal growth. He should derive some of these calories from 16 to 24 ounces of whole milk. (Low-fat milk should not be offered to a child under two years of age.)

From the Bottle

By the time your baby is a year old, you can begin to wean him from the bottle. Although infants can become very attached to the bottle, you can minimize this problem by not allowing your baby to hold it for extended periods of time. There is a difference between playing with the bottle and drinking from it. Because you have hopefully introduced the sippy cup months earlier, the transition from the bottle will be much easier. Begin by eliminating the bottle at one meal, substituting the cup. Then another meal, and another until the transition is completed. This may take anywhere from two weeks to a month. The time-table for this transition is set by Mom and Dad, not the baby.

We will close this section with a reminder. The more established a child's diet and eating routines are, based on parental direction and not the free will of the child, the smoother the process will go. Introducing solids to your baby's diet is part of the natural process of growth and development. Even with the introduction of solid foods, stay mindful to train your child so as to avoid retraining later - *begin as you mean to go.*

Chapter Four
Highchair Meals & Manners

W hen you add them up, your baby spends many hours a week in his or her highchair. Take advantage of this time by making it an opportunity for learning. As with many aspects of child development, there are both constant and variable influences to contend with. Parents are the constant influence on training. Whether at mealtime, playtime, or roomtime, parents should maintain a constant level of expectation regarding their child's behavior.

For example, the instructions "Do not drop your food" and "Do not touch the stereo," differ only in the nature of the activity, not in the level of parental expectation. The variable is the place or manner of offense, but the constant is the level of expectation. The "no" of the highchair should be the same as the "no" of the living room.

Parents of pretoddlers too often separate individual acts of behavior, rather than seeing their own need to be consistent as part of the same process. Although the settings and activities vary, parents should act as the constant influence, bringing to each situation the consistency necessary for orderly development and growth.

When a problem occurs at mealtime, consider any other conflicts that have taken place during the day. Are they related? Is the problem tied only to food, or does the child act similarly in other settings? For example, if your son is having trouble keeping his hands where they belong while he sits in his high-chair, is he also struggling with touching off-limit items in the living room? If so, the root problem is a general lack of self-control and not exclusively a mealtime weakness.

If you demand a standard at mealtime, then the same level of expectation must be in place at other times and with other activities. In the same way, if you demand compliance while in other settings but not at mealtime, confusion and frustration will result.

SELF-CONTROL TRAINING WITH HANDS

As a parent, you are an active participant in your child's advancing cognitive development (the process of learning how to put thoughts into action). It isn't wise to delay training in hopes that the process will get easier later on. Dealing with a problem "later" usually means backtracking. Make this your parenting motto: Train, don't retrain!

Baby and Mom will spend considerable time together at meals. For this reason, consider mealtime an opportunity to teach basic skills. For example, instruct your baby in the appropriate use of his hands and his voice, and begin to teach him early table manners. A baby learns by way of instruction and restriction. On the restrictive side, don't let him help you put pureed food into his mouth with his hands – the food usually ends up all over his face and in his hair. Also, he doesn't need to hold the utensil you're using to feed him. These are examples of behaviors that need to be restricted. Wrong habits learned early require correction later and that is unfair to the child.

If necessary, hold your baby's hands away from his food. Even better, teach him where to place his hands while being fed. You can start by having him place his hands on the side of the highchair tray or under the tray on his lap. There are advantages to this type of training. Training proactively now is better than training reactively in the future with correction. For example, the child who lacks hand control, first puts his fingers in his food, then in his hair, and then wipes them on his shirt resulting in the need for correction; often from a frustrated mother. She then has to start her training in the *negative*. Instead of introducing a new behavior she must first work to eliminate the unacceptable old patterns previously allowed.

That is why we emphasis; train in the way you mean to go now, so you are not spending more time correcting later. Do not allow a behavioral freedom that will eventually need to be corrected. In the example above, the mom isn't encouraging right behavior, she is only chasing after wrong behavior.

WHINING

Whining is an unacceptable form of communication that can become very annoying. It is a learned trait, not a warning of deep-seated emotional problems. At what age might whining begin? It can happen as soon as your child begins to communicate ideas. Though half-hearted at the outset and not done out of rebellion, whining will become either a bad habit or a tool of manipulation if not attended to early. The most common way parents reinforce this habit is by giving in to it.

Whining prior to fifteen months of age usually reflects a limited vocabulary. For example, if your baby wants more food, he or she may use a half-cry form of communication to ask for it. Although it is an expression of whining, it's not a protest or a challenge to authority at this stage. The good news is this: when you rightly deal with highchair whining, you are simultaneously hedging against behavioral whining that comes in the toddler and post-toddler years. You will be glad you worked on it early. Your friends and relatives will be too!

PROVIDING AN ALTERNATIVE

At these ages, the root problem is not the whining, but the lack of communication alternatives. Children between seven and twelve months of age have a growing capacity to communicate but not the verbal ability to do so. (For an expanded discussion on language development please see Appendix A.)

To prevent whining and to facilitate your child's acquisition of verbal skills, start to teach your seven month old a few words in sign language. It is never too early to emphasize "please" and "thank you". Remember, your child's verbal comprehension precedes his or her verbal vocabulary. You can effectively teach the following phrases: "please", "thank you", "stop", "more", and "all done".

Work on one expression at a time. You can actually start as early as six months by taking the child's hand through the motions while saying the word "please". Why "please?" Because "please" is one of the first acts of voluntary submission a child will give to his parent's leadership. It becomes the first courtesy and virtue that makes sense to the child and motivates him to do other virtues and courtesies.

Be consistent. Like all investments, the return on your training will come eventually. Depending on the child, it can take a few days or a few months. But, one day it will happen! Your baby will see some item that he desires and his little hand will begin to sign "please", knowing this action brings him rewards. Gradually, you can introduce "more" and "thank you", and expand from there.

Once your child reaches a year and you sense he under-

stands how to sign but refuses to do so, use natural consequences to reinforce the correct response. For example, if he
wants a toy but refuses to sign "please", withhold the toy. If it
is a cookie, withhold the cookie. However, try not to get into a
power struggle over food at mealtimes. You should not withhold
primary meals because your baby doesn't sign. In the context of
mealtime you might take his little hand and sign "please" with
him, saying to him, "let's do please" then give him his food.

You will have plenty of opportunity to work on sign language during the day other than mealtimes. Take advantage of
those opportunities. Here are some virtuous reasons to teach
basic sign language to your baby:

- You are teaching and reinforcing habits of self-control.

- Signing eliminates wrong communication methods by providing right modes of expression.

- Signing aids discretionary correction in the future. There
  will be times when you cannot easily correct your child
  publicly or verbally. The silence of signing, together with
  Mom's facial expression, communicates the same intent as
  verbal correction.

- You are actually teaching your child a second language during a time in the child's life when he or she is most receptive
  to language formation.

Don't be surprised if, when you initially begin by taking
your child's arm and hand to show the child what is required,
you feel resistance. This display of independence sometimes

51

can be clearly seen in a child as young as seven months of age. One mother shared her story describing how surprised she felt when her seven-month old daughter openly resisted Mom's attempts to teach her the "please" sign. She wrote:

"I was surprised when she resisted and actually tried to fight me. I realized this was one of the first battles that as a mother, I must win. I stayed with it, and in two week's time, my daughter was willingly and happily signing 'please' when she wanted something. Even more amazing was the lesson I learned; my child's surrender gave way to her own happiness." The child's ability to communicate amazed both her parents and other people who came into contact with her. "Now that she is twenty months old," the mother continued, "she signs 'please,' 'thank you,' 'more,' 'all done,' 'mommy,' 'daddy,' and 'I love you.' All this in addition to her developing verbal skills."

The benefits of early sign-training also pays dividends in the future. Three-year-old Eric, visiting the Ezzos, received a Valentine's Day treat from his host. The red foil wrapping paper immediately attracted Eric's attention. His Mom, standing behind the giver of the Valentine's Day chocolate, caught Eric's eye and discretely signed "thank you" to him. He in turn looked up at Mrs. Ezzo, and with a big grin said, "Thank you Mrs. Ezzo." This type of discretionary signing is far superior to the constant verbal reminder parents normally give, such as, "Eric, what do you say to Mrs. Ezzo?"

To teach your baby to sign is to teach him or her a second language. Like all new skills, the process of learning takes time, so please be patient. Your consistent effort and encouragement will pay big dividends. Start with the basics (the first four listed) and then gradually expand your child's signing vocabulary. Have fun!

PLEASE

Place right hand over heart and pull back toward right arm.

MORE

Use both hands, bring finger tips together and tap twice.

THANK YOU

Place tips of the hand (fingers together) against the mouth and throw hand forward, similar to blowing a kiss.

ALL DONE

Put hands in front of you with fingers spread apart. Turn hands back and forth.

DRINK

Place your hand in the shape of a "C" in front of mouth, thumb resting on chin, and bring hands up as if pouring a drink into the mouth.

EAT

All fingertips resting on thumb, bring hand toward mouth a couple of times.

THIRSTY

Slide tip of the index finger down front of neck.

HUNGRY

With hand in the shape of a "C," place it just below the throat, palm facing in, and bring it down.

MOMMY

With fingers spread apart, thumb touches middle of chin.

DADDY

With fingers spread apart, thumb touches middle of forehead.

YES

With hand in a fist, "nod" it back and forth. (Similar to nodding your head.)

NO

Bring index finger and middle finger together to rest on thumb in one "snapping" motions.

Section One Summary Points

Introducing Solids

1. A guiding principle: *Begin as you mean to go.*
2. Introduce solid foods between 4-7 months of age.
3. Introduce rice cereal first:
   a. Select a mealtime that is best for your family.
   b. Offer cereal three times a day.
   c. Breastfeed first – then offer cereal.
   d. Learning to take solids is a skill.
4. Introduce vegetables before introducing fruits.
   a. Introduce one new vegetable at a time.
   b. Wait three to four days and check for any possible allergic reaction.
5. Start introducing solids with your baby either in your arms or infant seat – eventually move child to the highchair.

Introducing Juices and Snacks

1. Introduce the sippy cup around 6 months of age.
2. Introduce juices between 6 and 8 months of age.
   a. Offer clear juices only, no pulp.
   b. Dilute juices 50-60% with water.
   c. Do not put baby down to sleep with a bottle of juice.
   d. Juice snacks are not substitute for meals.
3. Snacks and finger foods:
   a. Snacks do not have to be offered everyday.
   b. When offering snacks, do so between noon and dinner.
   c. Do not let your child wander around the house with snacks in hand.
4. Persevere with your family's favorite foods.
5. Try to breastfeed at least a year, but wean when Mom is ready.

6. Wean from bottle to the sippy cup around one year of age.

Highchair Meals and Manners

1. Self-control is a fundamental character quality for life.
2. Train in the way you mean to go rather than retrain with correction.
3. Paying attention to little hands:
    a. Mom should hold baby's hands when offering solids.
    b. Eventually train your baby to hold the side of high-chair tray.
    c. Instruct your pretoddler with emphasis placed on your tone of voice.
4. Introduce Sign Language:
    a. It can be used for all aspects of training.
    b. Sign Language helps curb whining in older children.
    c. Start with the "please" sign around 6 to 8 months and expect results around 11-12 months.
    d. Signing does not delay or hinder a child's speech development.

Section One — Questions for Review

1. Contrast the difference between the developmental concepts of growth and learning.

2. When should parents introduce the following into their baby's diet?:
   a. cereal

   b. vegetables

   c. finger foods

3. What wrong feeding habits disrupt your child's hunger patterns and sleep/wake stabilization? Explain.

4. How do you check for allergic reactions when introducing solid foods?

5. What are some safe and simple rules for introducing finger foods?

6. When and why should you introduce signing to your baby?

Section Two

Waketime & Nap Transitions

Chapter Five
Waketime Challenges

A llowing a pretoddler to grow up doing whatever he
wishes without placing any demands or limitations on
him, is not fair to the child. Children need a great deal
of guidance during these early months. This is a time of critical
learning. If parents set the right course for a child and encourage the child to stay on that course through caring parental
oversight, the child will be less likely to stray and more likely
to progress quickly through the process of learning. Waketime
challenges will come throughout the day and many times they
show up while your little one is sitting in his highchair.

Consider the following highchair challenges as opportunities for training. While the offenses listed below differ in action
(although they are related), the methods of correction for each
offense are often the same at these ages. Included in the group
of common highchair violations are:

- flipping the plate
- dropping and throwing food
- playing with food
- placing messy hands in his hair
- banging on the tray
- standing in the highchair
- arching his back
- spitting "raspberries"
- screaming

These behaviors share two things in common: they come during mealtime while the child is sitting in the highchair. Since eliminating mealtime is not an option, you will have to work on eliminating the highchair challenges. Let's consider two of them—flipping the plate and the intentional dropping of food from the highchair. When working to correct a new (but wrong) behavior, a bad habit, or better yet, to prevent one from starting, remember that correction is always consistent. Consistency aids the learning process, especially during the pretoddler stage.

FLIPPING THE PLATE AND DROPPING FOOD FROM THE HIGHCHAIR

Parents should place finger foods either directly on the highchair tray or on a plate. When finger foods are on a plate, one common and curious temptation of a child is to pick up the plate and flip it, spilling all the contents. Don't allow this to become a habit. Mealtime isn't playtime. A firm "No, do not touch your plate, only your food," is the starting point of training and correction. If you allow the child to play with the plate even though he or she doesn't spill the food, you have granted your child an unnecessary freedom. This freedom will only nudge him or her closer to wrong behavior and away from right behavior. There is no developmental advantage to be gained by allowing your child to play with a plate of food.

"But I don't want to stifle my child's creativity," is a commonly stated concern. Good news! Flipping food on the floor is not an act of creativity. It is wrong behavior. Creativity must be productive to be beneficial, not destructive.

Sometimes food is accidentally dropped. When that happens, guidance, not correction, is called for. But what about the intentional dropping or throwing of food from the highchair?

These actions need to be corrected. Some parents go to extremes to avoid conflict, rather than train their children in self-control. Believing a pretoddler is not capable of age-appropriate self-control tends to lead to behavioral freedoms that will require correction down the road. Whether it is with a pretoddler or a preschooler, this is known as "credit card parenting". You will pay the training price in the future, but with compound interest.

Instead of training a child not to drop food, some mothers allow the behavior and minimize damage by manipulating the child's environment. Inflating a child's vinyl swimming pool and placing it under the highchair is a good example. With this trick, the child can have fun with his or her food and the kitchen floor stays clean (until the child learns to throw food outside the perimeter of the pool). The mother has successfully avoided conflict—temporarily! But she is missing a wonderful opportunity to proactively train her child how to rightly behave in the highchair. This takes us back to our fundamental motto: *train, do not retrain.* Try to spend more time encouraging right behavior thereby spending less time correcting unwanted behaviors.

With this type of environmental manipulation, no urgency exists to train a child in appropriate mealtime self-control. Such an approach usually backfires on the parent. The self-control normally learned by properly handling food is the same self-control needed for life outside of the kitchen and for guiding the child later in life. Missed training opportunities result in slower intellectual growth and plenty of retraining.

You can train your baby not to drop food by giving immediate attention to the behavior. We will introduce some ideas about managing highchair challenges now and expand on them later in this chapter when we begin our discussion on the various "Methods of Correction".

The first thing a parent should do when dealing with the habitual plate flipper is to verbally express to the baby this is a "No" behavior. Next, you might add an attention-getting squeeze to the baby's hand while pointing out what that little hand just did. The operative phrase is "attention-getting". Your intent is not to cause pain for the purpose of punishment but rather give a slight discomfort to get the child's attention so you can train him to your level of mealtime expectation.

Finally, if your instructions are ignored, isolate him or her in the crib. The child will fuss over this consequence, but when the isolation period is finished, bring him or her back to the highchair and try again. If the child persists in the behavior (and some will), mealtime may be over and naptime begins. One thing is for certain: immediate and consistent consequences speed up the learning process. In the past, educators were concerned with parents who pushed their children too fast. Today, we are concerned with parents who do not push their children fast enough when it comes to proper moral training.

The principles of correction for flipping a plate or dropping food are also the same for the rest of the highchair offenses listed earlier. For example, the child who plays with his food (mashing it needlessly), stands in his highchair, or bangs his spoon on his tray receives first a verbal correction, using a calm but firm voice and, if needed, isolate to the crib. Possibly, lunchtime is over for now. Again, your choices are limited by your child's age.

If the child is blowing bubbles with his food (commonly referred to as blowing "raspberries"), lightly place your finger over the child's mouth and give a stern, "No! Keep your food in your mouth." If further correction is needed, isolation is usually the next step. You can expect your child to respond to these methods of correction with positive results.

THE IMPORTANCE OF VERBAL INSTRUCTION

You may wonder how much of your instructions your baby can comprehend or understand. The answer? Probably more than you think. Your child is really beginning to blossom with understanding in the later months of his first year. Let's look at the three phases of vocabulary comprehension and mastery.

Understanding vocabulary is the first phase. That is, a child understands the meanings of words long before he or she can verbalize them. Your six-month-old will wave "bye-bye" or play "patty cake" when encouraged to do so by you. By eight months of age, your child has an enormous understanding of vocabulary and demonstrates this by his or her responses to instructions such as "Come to Mama", "Sit down", "Blow kisses", "Hug your baby doll", "See the plane", "Touch the kitty", "Wave bye-bye", and so on. Your child is responding with understanding, but hasn't yet learned to speak the words he or she understands.

Speaking vocabulary is the second level of achievement, and usually develops around twelve months of age. Your baby will begin to babble to a toy or sibling at this age. Though we may not understand it, this babbling means something to your child. They are word-thoughts coming out in scrambled speech representing your baby's attempt to communicate with language.

Reading vocabulary is the third level of achievement. It begins after age three, when a child starts to recognize and form letters. (For an expanded explanation of language development, see Appendix A.)

Your baby comes into this world ready to learn. That is why you can teach exactly what you expect through instruction. For example, as we previously introduced, you can train your baby where to put his hands during mealtime. Take and place them either on the side of the highchair tray or underneath the tray on baby's lap. Verbally instruct him with "Put your hands on the side of the tray, please," while actually taking his hands and placing them where you want them to be.

Concrete example along with verbal instruction will move your little person in the direction you wish him to go. The benefits of this type of training goes far beyond your child knowing where to place his hands on the highchair at mealtime. Your pretoddler is actually following your instructions. This is a milestone in and of itself. Training right habits is better and easier than correcting poor habits. Be patient with your child, but above all, be proactive. Your baby understands more than you think.

Speaking to Your Baby by Name

In the instructing and correcting process, parents tend to direct their baby with specific statements. "Place your hands on the side of the highchair" or "Don't drop your food" are two examples. Can parents improve on these instructions? We believe they can and should. Preempt your instructions with your child's name, saying "Matthew, place your hands on the side of the highchair please" or "Matthew, do not drop your food." Because infants are by nature *me* oriented, saying his name while giving your instruction draws attention to the specific task you're looking to accomplish. Think it through. When there is a fun item we want our baby to observe we almost naturally begin with the child's name; "Matthew, look at the balloon". We do this because we want him to focus specifically on the balloon. The same principle works with your instruction.

Yet, even this simple suggestion will change in less than a year's time as Matthew approaches his second birthday. For mid-toddlers and preschoolers, instructions start with the child's name, followed by a pause. Here Mom is looking for an acknowledgement, nod of the head, or a verbal "Yes, Mommy". Only after that is received will you proceed with your instructions. For example, Mom might call, "Matthew". Matthew responds to his name, "Yes Mommy", after which Mom gives the instruction, "Pick up your toys please, and put them in your box." In early parenting you will want to establish in Matthew's mind your right to be the authority in his life. The instructions you give are secondary to Matthew's willingness to respond to your voice seeking his attention. Get that first, and you usually end up having your instructions followed with far less resistance, if any at all.

The foundation for healthy instruction and responses begin early, and starts with your baby's name. Keep in mind that it is a process and you are taking "baby steps" toward the goal of a well-adjusted and responsive child.

METHODS OF CORRECTION

Parents are responsible for training. The word *train* means "to initiate," "get started," "set the patterns," and "cause one to learn." The goal of pretoddler training is not to prevent your child from exploring life, but to help him or her develop healthy behavior patterns that will enable the child to learn about life.

Those patterns include paying attention, focusing and concentrating on what he or she is doing—all fundamental skills of life your child will need before he starts school. You began the process with your basic routine, and will continue in it by encouraging your child in right behavior and by correcting wrong behavior.

In the pretoddler phase, behaviors needing correction are initially wrong functionally but not morally. By that we mean young children need correction for inappropriate actions, but parents must realize they are not truly dealing with heart attitudes because pretoddlers do not think in terms of right and wrong, nor are they capable of making such judgments. Nonetheless, parents still need to correct wrong patterns and encourage right patterns.

The Highchair

The very need for this specific type of baby furniture assumes your baby has the physical ability to sit up for an extended period of time and is old enough to associate his behavior with your responses. Therefore, the right method of correction and appropriate limits needed to achieve your training goals must correspond to your child's physical ability and age-appropriate understanding. The following recommendations are for children who are ten months and older. At this age the normal highchair problems (and other problem areas) are solved by the following methods of correction. You can correct with:

1. Verbal Correction. Direct with your voice, speaking firmly but not harshly. Please keep in mind that the "voice of urgency" is not the same as the "voice of harshness". Sometimes an elevated voice tone will be necessary.

2. A light to moderate squeeze to the hand. It's a fact—discomfort gets any human's attention faster than anything else. Applying moderate discomfort as a method of correction is reserved for the older, more mobile child whose hands are touching things they shouldn't be. It is not used as a punishment, but as an attention-getting device. A slight squeeze on the hand, when accompanied by verbal correction acts as a deterrent to wrong behaviors that are not safe. Using such methods for the express purpose of calling attention to a limitation will not leave your child psychologically damaged, affect the child's self-esteem, train the child to hit other children, teach the child violence, or cause the child in adulthood to abuse his or her own children. But they will instill a healthy sense of self-restriction.

3. Loss of a privilege or toy. This is a logical consequence that also works effectively. The purpose of logical consequences is to reinforce your verbal instructions.

4. Isolation in the crib or playpen. Simply put, this means removing the child from an act or place of conflict and putting the child in his or her crib. A ten month old can very quickly learn cause-and-effect relationships. He can also learn that behavioral expectations are not negotiable.

Note: Spanking, as traditionally practiced in our society, is not an acceptable form of correction during the pretoddler phase of development. If you intend to introduce it into the life of your child it will be at a much later age. For now, it's enough to say that the use of verbal reprimands, isolation, loss of privilege, and squeezing the hand are appropriate disciplines during the second half of the baby's first year and right up until eighteen months of age.

Chapter Six
Waketime Activities

I n the building process, whether it be for a physical structure or the moral fabric of a human heart, it is vital to lay
the proper foundation. Unfavorable or inadequate training
even as young as six months of age can seriously sabotage physical and mental development. This is why the establishment
of right patterns of behavior is basic to all human potential.
Parents must not only give attention to what is imparted, but
also to how it is imparted.

Establishing right learning patterns plays an increasingly
dominant role in the five to twelve month old's development.
Right patterns ultimately affect the way a child manages instruction, direction, correction, limitation, freedom, and new and
growing relationships. As he or she grows, the child's world
develops and becomes increasingly more complex. Therefore,
how a baby assimilates knowledge and learns to respond to
parental cues are foundational to all future growth.

WHAT YOUR BABY'S BRAIN REALLY NEEDS
Some parents think they can stuff knowledge in their infant's
developing brain like a Deli-master stuffs a bratwurst. Plopping
your infant in front of a television set for his daily regime of
"brain stimulating" videos or attempting to teach your eight-
month-old math and Swahili will not make the way for your
"little genius" or create the world's next Einstein. Far from it.

As well-intentioned as many parents may be to push their baby to the front of the class, their emphasis is in the wrong place—on knowledge stimulation rather than developing a healthy infrastructure for learning. Helping to stimulate an efficient knowledge processing system during the critical first year and-a-half is a "must-attain" goal for pretoddler parenting. Videos for babies hinders this process.

The outcry against marketing educational videos to parents of infants has now reached the federal level with complaints filed with the Federal Trade Commission (FTC) responsible for overseeing false advertisement (May 11, 2006). Research strongly suggests that television viewing for babies is negatively associated with cognitive development, regular sleep patterns, and time spent interacting with parents and engaged in creative play. Television viewing can also be habit-forming and, for older children, is linked to childhood obesity and poor school performance.

Published studies in the August 8, 2007 edition of the Journal of Pediatrics confirms that every hour infants spend watching baby videos is associated with slower language development. Children exposed to videos as babies score lower on standardized vocabulary tests than children who didn't watch videos at all. The American Academy of Pediatrics (AAP) guidelines recommend children under the age of two watch no television and no screen entertainment, including computer images.

There's little debate among educational clinicians that a child's ability to learn is tied to how the brain organizes information and what stimulates thoughts, ideas and answers. Structuring learning opportunities into your child's day aids the process, while overloading the senses with random images impedes it. Your pretoddler's brain is not set up for the type of single direction, passive learning that comes from multicolored video animations, regardless of how a product is marketed or what it promises. Colorful, fast-moving and bouncing images filling a screen do not facilitate optimal brain organization and actually work against it.

All children (especially infants), need two-way human inter-action that comes from Mom and Dad. Your baby needs to hear your voice, participate in conversation and have songs directed at him or her while cuddling, nursing or playing. Your baby's brain is interacting far more with the real thing; that being Mom and Dad than with a thirty-two inch screen. It is this type of stimulation that facilitates better brain organization. More senses are stimulated, including sight, sound, smell and touch, as well as the warm, loving feeling associated with the protective environment of Mom and Dad's arms.

Talk, talk, talk to your baby while feeding, playing, dress-ing, walking or riding in the car. Use adult language, not baby talk. Read to your baby everyday. Stimulate your pretoddler's memory skills through infant games like peek-a-boo and patty-cake and practice waving "bye-bye". Get siblings and Grandma and Grandpa involved. You can help your baby develop eye-hand coordination by providing age-appropriate toys, such as blocks or anything that is safe that he can manipulate with his hands. Even a couple of clean pot holders will do the trick.

The point here is the human-factor cannot be replaced or outsourced. Educational videos for infants are a clear contradic-tion. The more the responsive side of the brain is left unattended during video input, the less organized the brain becomes and the greater the potential increase for learning disorders, includ-ing a deficiency in focusing and concentrating skills. This is in part due to the single fact that screen images are always moving. The child is not learning anything because his brain is not developed sufficiently to receive colorful, fast moving objects. There is no pre-existing understanding to tie those images to anything.

Mozart Effect and Classical Music

Filling the airways of your home with classical music as a way of providing an educational edge to infants and toddlers is another topic of contemporary interest. In research circles, this is known as the "Mozart Effect." The Mozart Effect was based on a study done in 1993 which suggested that listening to Mozart could increase one's spatial reasoning (aiding logic). But hang on. Before rushing out to pick up music by your favorite classical composer, understand the research was done on college students, not babies. The research was not thorough although the findings had some qualified value and theoretical credibility.

None-the-less, music is a unique language because it has the ability to completely bypass the listener's mind and speak directly to his heart. We know that classical music is very orderly in its construction and through its order can convey a peaceful spirit. This is particularly true of the music composed by Bach and Mozart.

Man has the ability to listen to music on two levels. On the surface, we hear a song and its melody. Below the surface, but just above the subconscious level, we hear the logic of the melody. It is theorized that when young children are exposed to classical music, the logic center of the brain is strengthened and those areas dependent on logic (mathematics and complex reasoning skills) are reinforced. While there is some evidence supporting this conclusion, none of it is linked to music videos or flashing images tied to a screen as mentioned in the beginning of this chapter.

To what extent babies can relate to expressions of logic (through the medium of music) is not known at this time. But they do relate to orderliness and routine which are, in the end, expressions of the creative order of things.

DEVELOPMENTAL DEPRIVATION

The term "developmental deprivation" doesn't refer to a child's being deprived of opportunities to learn, but of the best opportunities to learn. To a large extent, a child's environment determines his learning patterns. We believe learning deprivation occurs when parents consider their child's impetuous and momentary desires to be their prime source of learning. For example, allowing a child to crawl or walk around the house without any guidelines, directions, or restrictions, represents a dubious channel of learning. Learning this way is too often accidental and outside the context of the pretoddler's developing world.

The nonrestrictive theory of allowing a child to explore unhindered is the idea that learning through trial-and-error in a non-structured environment, (where parents merely act as facilitators of learning rather than teachers of knowledge) is a superior training method. This is not true! Far from it! Trial-and-error self-exploration is inferior to structured guidance with proactive teaching. Allowing trial-and-error learning to become the primary source of education for a young child, is time-consuming and too often the end results are far from satisfactory. Trial-and-error parenting often creates learning environments that are greater in scope than the intellectual capacities of the child and fosters behavior patterns that will require retraining later.

Children need direction and guidance from their parents. They must learn correct, specific responses for specific situations and then be able to transfer the concept learned to other settings. "Do not drop your food" and "Do not touch the stereo" are two examples. While the actions are different, the desired response to both is the same—submission to parental instruction and leadership.

If parents reinforce their instruction in the kitchen but not in the living room, the child's ability to discriminate between what is expected and what is allowed becomes clouded. (More specifics on this aspect of training can be found in the Topic Pool category: "Baby Proofing: Yes or No?")

PLANNED LEARNING OPPORTUNITIES

Learning opportunities should be predominantly the result of planning, not chance. The establishment of healthy learning patterns is the result of providing the right learning environment, one in which controlled stimuli (those factors that normally call for curiosity and investigation) are part of your baby's day. To achieve this end, plan some structured time into your baby's waketime. These opportunities will include: 1) structured playtime alone, 2) time with family members, and 3) free playtime.

Structured Playtime Alone

We maintain that play serves the learning process. The spontaneous interest of pretoddlers is not the only influence on their play, since parents control, to a large extent, the environment in which their child learns. For this reason, both structured and nonstructured learning environments are needed. Structured playtime is a specific time during the day when a child has time to play by himself or herself. It starts in the early months with something as simple as a blanket placed on the floor/carpet where Mom can see the baby, but the baby cannot see Mom. This is called "Blanket-time". Blanket-time will eventually be coupled with (but not be replaced by) "Playpen-time". The next transition after that is "Roomtime" (18 to 22 months). The principles of roomtime are the same as for the playpen, but you will be using the child's room as his or her play area.

BLANKET-TIME

Sometimes when we look at a baby, it is hard to imagine that a six-month-old, laying on his tummy on a small blanket with a colorful teething ring is doing much more than passing time. To the contrary, blanket-time facilitates learning by providing a secluded environment that allows baby to focus and concentrate apart from distracting sights and sounds in the house.

Introduce blanket-time before your baby becomes mobile. (Even if you introduce blanket-time after your baby is crawling, he can still learn to stay on the blanket, although Mom will have some additional training to keep him there.) With consistency, your baby will learn to stay within the boundaries of the blanket. Although the baby will soon transition to playpen-time, there will always be an occasion when blanket-time will be Mom and baby's friend.

Where to Begin

Blanket-time starts as soon as your baby is able to hold his head up and manipulate his hands on a object. This can be as early as four months of age. Start with five to ten minute increments once a day and stretch the times to a level tolerated by your baby. The beauty of a blanket is it's mobility. You can place it just about anywhere in the house where it is convenient for Mom and Dad. Even grandparents will find it helpful when baby is over for a visit.

PLAYPEN-TIME

Technically, you will not transition from blanket-time to the playpen. A transition assumes leaving one item or phase of learning and moving to another. While "playpen-time" will become more and more dominant for your child and the greater focus of Mom and Dad's attention, it does not mean "blanket-time" will become obsolete. Once your baby is characterized by staying on the blanket, it can be used anywhere necessary because the blanket travels easier than a pack-and-play or play-pen. There will always be that occasion when at the Doctor's office, while visiting a friend, at picnics, even while Mom and Dad are in a meeting, when baby can benefit from some "alone" time rather than "lap-time".

One of the great benefits of blanket-time is how it leads right into playpen-time. Here are some playpen advantages:

It provides a safe environment. Playpens are a safe place to put your baby when your attention must be elsewhere and it's not the baby's naptime. Playpens enable you to take a shower, unload groceries from the car, care for other children, and do a host of other activities—all the while knowing your child is safe.

It doubles as a portable bed. The playpen can serve as a portable bed, which is especially useful when visiting in another family's home. The playpen gives the baby a clean, familiar place to sleep.

It offers a structured learning center. The partnership a child has with the playpen establishes foundational intellectual skills. Planned daily playpen times allow little ones the opportunity to develop in many ways.

Benefits of the Playpen

- It aids focusing skills. Playpen time helps a child develop the ability to concentrate on an object or activity at hand and not be constantly distracted.

- It aids sustained attention span. You will observe how your child picks up a toy, manipulates it with his or her hands, examines it carefully, shakes it, and then repeats the process again.

- It aids creativity. Creativity is the product of boundaries, not freedom. With absolute freedom, there is no need for creative thinking or problem-solving.

- It aids self-play adeptness. This is one of the positive signs that your baby is moving from dependence to independence.

- It aids orderliness. The first step to developing orderliness is to help your child with cleanup times. Start by placing a few books in one corner, a bucket of small toys in another, or stacking other items in a neat pile. Simple statements such as "Let's put the toys in the basket," or "Help Mommy clean up," aid the process. The object is to leave the area neat, with the child participating in achieving that goal.

If the child misses structured playtime, the repertoire of skills he might otherwise attain by these activities could be seriously delayed or compromised. The playpen is all about creating the right learning environment.

When to Use the Playpen

Schedule your playpen-times at approximately the same time(s) each day, selecting times when your baby is fresh and alert (not before naptime, for example). Put one or two interesting toys within the baby's reach, or put the toys in a small basket and place the basket in the playpen. Keep the toys age-appropriate, and occasionally rotate them. The child who finds a shiny blue rattle fascinating at five months of age will ignore it at ten months of age. Local libraries carry books that describe the types of toys or activities your baby is likely to be interested in at each stage of development.

One important aspect of selecting appropriate toys is understanding what is not a toy. Tools, markers, mechanical devices, and Mom or Dad's private and personal property are not toys. Mom's earrings, billfold, and lipstick in her purse (and the purse itself, for that matter) are not toys. Neither is Dad's pocket pen, reading glasses or hammer. Think about it! If you amuse your baby with general and personal items now, will these same play items be off limits in a few months? If they will not be appropriate toys then, should they be allowed now?

If you have twins, alternate their times in the playpen. Put one in the playpen in the morning, the other in it in the afternoon. Occasionally try putting them both in at the same time. If your home allows for it, vary the location of the playpen from time to time. For example, during the week you might put it in the living room. Then on the weekend, place it near the sliding glass door overlooking the backyard, where the child's siblings are playing. In warm weather, take the playpen outside.

Position the playpen so you can easily check on your baby, but where your child cannot see you. It detracts from the purpose of self-focusing playtime if the child can see Mom or Dad. Forcing a child to, in effect, choose between creative self-play or Mom sitting in the next room is not fair to him. If you live in a small apartment, be creative. For example, you might use a portable room divider to section off part of the living room or bedroom.

The time your baby spends in the playpen will vary with age. During the first few months, your baby should have ten to twenty minutes twice a day in the playpen. By the time your baby can sit by himself or herself, you can extend playpen-time to fifteen to thirty minutes, twice a day. Once your baby starts to crawl, increase the time to thirty to forty-five minutes at least once a day. Between fifteen and twenty months, your child can play up to one hour either in the playpen or possibly in his or her room. These are suggested guidelines, of course. Some days your child will play for longer periods in the playpen, and he will play for shorter intervals on other days.

We offer words of caution and encouragement: Don't overuse the playpen by leaving your baby in it for extended and unplanned periods during the day. "Playpen-time" normally should be a planned activity, not an all-day event.

As a word of encouragement, children of all ages have a love/hate relationship with boundaries. They hate boundaries simply because they are there, yet they love them because of the security they provide. That's true of the playpen. If your child doesn't appear to like the playpen at first, stay with five minutes until he accepts it. Rest assured, the playpen will become a fun place for him.

Keeping the Timer Handy

The use of a timer is very beneficial when first starting play-pen training. Whether your child adapts with perfect calm or cries in protest, you want him to learn when the timer goes off, the activity is over. It is better that a child associates the end of his playpen-time with the timer's ring than with his persistent crying. If a timer is not used, the baby/child will cry without ceasing, thinking their crying is what brings Mom or Dad in to them. Do not let that happen. It is not fair to the child to think crying will get him everything he wants.

Starting Late

How should you introduce the playpen if it hasn't been part of your baby's day prior to this? Again, training starts with a timer! If your baby is not used to boundaries, any adjustment will probably bring tears of protest. When they come, you have a decision to make. Give in to the child or direct him based on what is best for the child. Start with short periods of time—maybe five to ten minutes a day. Over the next two or three weeks, work up to twenty minutes then thirty. After a month, extend the time to forty-five minutes. In time your child will love his playpen time and so will you. If there is any crying, the advantages gained outweigh a few tears.

LEARNING TIMES WITH FAMILY MEMBERS

There are some obvious activities which take place during wake-time that include interaction with one or more family members. While enjoying your relationship with your pretoddler, it is important to find the right balance between playing with your child and becoming your child's sole source of entertainment.

If you begin to find that your child clings to you, refuses to go to Dad or siblings and cries when you leave the room, it may be the result of too much play time with Mom and not enough time with other family members. Of course, we would hope that every mom has play time with her child, but never to the point where the child begins to shut out other family members. To help prevent this, keep your activities family-centered. Here are a few suggestions.

<u>Reading</u>: It's never too early to read to your baby or to show him colorful picture books (especially cardboard or plastic ones that he or she can explore alone). This is a fun activity for older siblings and Dad to be part of. Pretoddlers enjoy being read to long before they can understand the words. The continuous flow of sound and the changes in vocal inflections and facial expressions attract a child's attention. Nestling your child in your lap when you read further enhances this experience.

<u>Bathing</u>: This is another opportunity to have fun interaction with your baby. You can sing to your baby, talk to him, and ask him questions such as, "Where is Matthew's ear?" or "Where is Matthew's arm?" or "Where is Matthew's hand?" and then respond, "Here is Matthew's ear.", "Here is Matthew's arm." and "Here is Matthew's hand." Mom, Dad, and even the older siblings' voice and attention plays a big part in helping your baby understand the intimate world of family relationships.

<u>Walking:</u> Taking time for a stroll outside is a great activity for the family. By six months of age, your baby becomes fascinated with the treasure of God's creation. A regular walk becomes a big adventure for your child, and it is healthy for you too.

<u>Touching:</u> A healthy influence on a child's emotional develop-

ment is the type of physical touching that comes through play activities. Play is an important part of a child's growth. Touch communicates intimacy, and together, touch and play form a winning combination. Lying down on the couch, floor, or bed and blowing kisses, tickling, and physically playing with your baby are necessary components in the formation of a healthy relationship.

SUMMARY

The type of behavioral adjustments a child makes in life are greatly influenced by the child's understanding of his or her environment, other people, and awareness of self. Waketime activities serve growth and development. But these activities need to be organized rather than become free-for-all experiences which fall between meals and naps. When a child receives guidance in establishing right patterns of behavior, learning is advanced.

Chapter Seven

Nap Transitions and Nighttime Sleep

⌒⌐⌐⌐⌐⌐⌒

A s stated in *Babywise,* where there is ability there is a natural capacity. Your baby has already demonstrated both the natural capacity and ability to sleep through the night, which is an acquired skill resulting from training. This chapter focuses on sleep-related activities and the various sleep transitions. Our next chapter answers the most common nap and sleep questions related to this stage of growth.

THE SLEEP TRANSITIONS

Stable sleep patterns are based on stable hunger patterns. When there are a number of disruptions in your baby's eating or wake-time patterns, there will be corresponding changes in his sleep patterns. Stay on top of this by being consistent as possible with mealtime and naptime. Sleep is an important part of a baby's life, and it will continue to be throughout the toddler years.

Dropping the Late Afternoon Nap

For optimal development, children need daytime rest. For the *Babywise* mom, the procedure is fairly simple. When naptime comes, baby goes down. Not much will change over the next twelve months. At five months of age, the average *Babywise* baby takes two, 1 1/2 to 2-hour naps and an additional "cat-nap" in the late afternoon. Between six and eight months of age, his sleep needs decrease, as his waketime increases. This is especially noticeable in babies who sleep ten to twelve hours at night. The "sleep-center" in a baby's brain will begin to send an "awake signal" if there is too much sleep in a 24-hour period. That is when you know your baby is ready to drop his afternoon "cat-nap". (For an expanded discussion on naps and nighttime sleep, please see Chapter Eight.)

How will you know when your baby is ready to drop another nap? Here are the three common signs:

1. Your baby begins waking in the middle of the night.

2. Your baby is waking very early in the morning.

3. Your baby is routinely waking early during one or both daytime naps, possibly sleeping only 45 minutes.

Be cautious. The signs above are not exclusively associated with nap transitions. Other factors may mirror these symptoms, including hunger, sickness or possibly teething. All possibilities must be considered before acting on any single factor. If it is sleep related, drop the cat-nap first. This sleep transition may also require you to adjust the morning nap by pushing it back thirty to forty-five minutes, creating a longer morning waketime.

Your baby will continue with two naps a day until the next sleep transition around sixteen to twenty months of age, when the morning nap is dropped. We'll cover this transition in the next book dealing specifically with the toddler years.

"Wake-up Happy Rule"
A parent's belief about sleep highly influences a baby's wake-

up disposition. A well-rested baby has a happy disposition. He will make cooing sounds and play in the crib, letting you know it is time to get him up. This happy outcome can be yours if you follow three basic rules for naptime.

Rule One: Mom, not baby, decides when the nap starts.

Rule Two: Mom, not baby, decides when the nap ends.

Rule Three: If your baby wakes up crying or cranky, it is most likely because he has not had sufficient sleep.

There are other reasons babies wake up before a full nap is achieved. Your baby might be moving into the next nap transition, he might be hungry, has a soiled diaper, is showing early signs of sickness, an arm or leg is stuck in a crib slat, or on occasion, a noisy neighbor or siblings disrupt him. This is when parental assessment comes into play. If none of the descriptions above fit, then you have a decision to make. Either get your baby up and readjust his schedule or consider leaving him in his crib (even with a little fussing or crying), and hope he falls back to sleep for another thirty to forty minutes.

Another option is to go in and gently pat his back for a few moments, reassuring him that you hear him. A third option is to pick him up and cuddle for a few minutes, calming him down and then return him to his crib. If he continues to fuss after this, maybe naptime is over for today. Readjust his schedule for the rest of the day and monitor tomorrow's sleep-times.

The Fatigued Baby
The question is not all that uncommon: "My perfect six-

month-old sleeper is fighting his naps to the point of fatigue. He is so over-tired that he can't sleep. Should I just let him "cry it out?" The correct answer depends on whether the question is related to a "tired" baby or a "fatigued" baby. The fatigued baby is a uniquely different challenge than the tired baby.

The most important lesson to learn from this scenario is knowing that the character traits of *infant fatigue* are not the same as those of a *tired baby*. The tired baby can usually recoup the sleep needed in one "good" nap or at least within a 24-hour cycle. The fatigued baby actually has a disruption in the sleep cycles that requires special attention.

If you keep your baby up and he skips his naps, the problem will only get worse. If you attempt to force sleep on the child, by not responding to his cries (legitimately born out of fatigue), Mom and Dad can quickly become emotional wrecks and your baby will not be helped.

Let's look into the context and uniqueness of this challenge. For the *Babywise* baby, healthy sleep has two primary components that most moms are unwilling to give up. The child who sleeps through his naps without waking, and the child who sleeps in his crib for those naps. While both are important, one must be temporarily suspended for the greater good of the baby. By greater good we mean the restoration of his natural sleep rhythms. How will you accomplish this?

Infant fatigue is not much different than adult fatigue. We all know what it feels like to be so tired that you can't sleep. That's because fatigue attacks the sleep rhythms, preventing a child from entering the ebb and flow of active and relax sleep states. It may come as a result of a baby's routine being out of whack for several days, especially during the time of day when naps are a normal part of the baby's day. The priority is for Mom to find a non-stressful solution to re-establishing her baby's circadian rhythm.

If the nap challenge is fatigue and you know you can get him back into a predictable routine, we recommend Mom find a comfortable chair, a good book, sit down and allow that baby to take his nap in her arms. This might extend into the next day. On the third day, however, naps return to the crib.

Does this work? Yes, most definitely. It works because the tension between the need for sleep and the place for sleep is temporarily suspended while baby is getting restorative sleep. Yet, you are not creating a sleep prop because this sleep adjustment is for a couple of days, and you are satisfying his real sleep need by helping him overcome the fatigue.

Prevention is, of course, the best medicine. It always is, and it always will be. Try to think through how your perfect sleeper became a fatigued baby. It didn't just happen, and one day's suspension of a baby's routine will not foster the condition of fatigue. Two or three days of continual disruption may. Take a look at what is going on in your home and with the baby's schedule and make the appropriate adjustments.

Do not take this sleep challenge lightly. Optimal alertness comes from optimal sleep. It is during the time of optimal alertness that your baby's brain grows and develops. Poor sleep habits negatively impact the brain's neuro-chemical transmitters that stimulate growth.

Nighttime Sleep

At six months of age, your baby's nighttime sleep patterns should be well-established. Usually an average of ten to twelve hours of continuous sleep should be the norm. These patterns will change little over the next eighteen months except for a few temporary disruptions due to sickness or daytime nap transitions.

SLEEP PROPS AND PROBLEMS
Sleep is a natural function of the body. The primary cue for infant sleep is sleepiness. Sleep cues are influenced (often negatively) by a variety of sleep-associated props. Some sleep props, such as a special blanket or stuffed animal are usually harmless, while others, such as the nighttime bottle, pacifier, and thumb-sucking, can be addictive. The problem with sleep props is not getting the child to fall asleep initially, but helping him learn to fall back to sleep without the prop. Here are a few of them.

The Bottle
The most common sleep prop for the older baby is the nighttime bottle. Too many children become conditioned to going to bed with a bottle and depend on it to fall asleep. You can avoid the bottle prop by not getting in the habit of putting your baby down with one. This does not mean he will never take a bottle in his crib. There may be an occasional nap when baby, bottle, and crib form a convenient alliance for a busy mom. As long as this behavior does not become habit-forming, it will not become addictive.

The Blanket
So that your child does not become overly attached to one blanket, consider limiting its use to the crib/bed and on some occasions a long car ride. Do not let your baby or pretoddler drag it everywhere he goes. Although using the same blanket provides a sense of familiarity, true security is tied to relationships with Mom and Dad, not objects.

The Pacifier

There are many good reasons for using a pacifier with your newborn. But by six months of age, any need for additional non-nutritive sucking is greatly diminished. Does your child need a pacifier to fall asleep? If so, now is the time to start thinking about breaking this habit.

Experience and common sense teach that it is easier to remove the pacifier at six months than at twelve or eighteen months of age. It works best to remove it gradually. You might try putting your baby down for one nap without his pacifier. See how that goes. Eventually move to the other naps and then nighttime. Might there be some crying? Consider yourself fortunate if there isn't some cry of protest. We assure you the crying will be temporary.

Another suggestion is to pierce the pacifier with a needle and release the vacuum. The vacuum bubble is what makes the pacifier enjoyable; when the bubble is gone, the pleasure is decreased, often resulting in the child weaning himself from his "binky". This suggestion can be applied to the six-month-old or sixteen-month-old.

Sudden and Unexplainable Cry

It's scary! Your baby cries as if in pain but you do not know why. First, you check the forehead for any indication of a fever. Ears and nose are next. No redness is good news so you examine the baby's mouth for an emerging new tooth. Nothing there. Examination time is over. You assume it is a sleep issue.

Not so fast! The sudden and unexplainable cry has reason, and as a parent you must figure out why. If you haven't already, get into the habit of checking your baby over once a day, including fingers and toes. There is a condition, though relatively under-reported, called 'toe-tourniquet' syndrome. A single strand of hair, usually Mom's, or a fiber from a shagged carpet where the baby was playing somehow gets wrapped around a toe or finger. Although hardly noticeable, it eventually begins to tighten and cut off circulation to the appendage, causing swelling, inflammation, and pain. The problem is often missed because the baby is wearing a sock or sleeper. While this may not explain every sudden and unexplainable cry, it does alert you to the need for a daily "once over" of your baby's body.

Chapter Eight
Questions About Sleep

W hen it comes to babies and pretoddlers, there are a few disruptions that can turn a great nap and nighttime sleeper into a challenging child. But rest assured, most challenges can be explained and brought under control. While few in number, the questions below address the most common challenges relating to naps and nighttime sleep for babies between five and twelve months old.

1. Our six-month-old has always slept through the night. Now all of a sudden he is waking and crying. Why is this happening? What should we do?

   This is not an uncommon problem and can occur any time between five and eight months. There are four common reasons why babies wake at night.

One: The first reason is hunger. His waking may be a signal that he is ready for solid foods, or if you are breastfeeding, your milk supply may not be keeping up with your baby's nutritional needs, or he may be going through a growth spurt. (If this is the case add another one or two nursing periods during the day or you might supplement with a bottle after breastfeeding.)

Two: The second reason is associated with the third nap (late afternoon). It may be time to drop it. With three full naps a day, your baby may be getting too much sleep.

Three: The third reason babies wake at night is teething, or sickness. This is easier to identify since daytime irritability usually accompanies this condition.

Four: The fourth reason is associated with disruption in your baby's daytime routine. Has there been a major change in it? Has this been a busy week? Are you working part-time? Is your baby being overly entertained by friends and relatives or co-workers to the point that naps are being skipped? Overtired babies are fussy when they are laid down. Do you have relatives visiting who feel it is their responsibility to hold your baby all day? Are you just getting back from a long trip? Evaluate the possible sources of the problem and make the appropriate changes knowing it might take two or three days to get him back on track. Do what you must to protect your baby's naptime.

2. Our six-month-old baby is sleeping fine at night but all of a sudden is waking forty-five minutes into each nap. Is this normal? Should we get him up?

It is not uncommon for *Babywise* babies between five and eight months old, to begin waking halfway through their naps and give the appearance of being ready to get up. The reasons cited in Question One all apply to your nap challenges as well. To that list you can add a heightened sense of alertness that is just part of your baby's normal growth.

In *Babywise*, we discussed the rotating Relaxed Sleep Patterns (RSP) and the Active Sleep Patterns (ASP). As your child comes out of his first relaxed sleep state which is about forty-five minutes into his nap, his new sense of alertness is affected by familiar sounds. It could be the sound of a door shutting, the furnace going on, the school bus outside bringing home siblings, or a host of other familiar noises. The alertness seems to trigger curiosity and instead of falling back to sleep, he wakes and calls for you.

If this is the case, your baby still needs to learn how to fall back to sleep and not let his curiosity control his sleep patterns. Check to make sure everything is okay, but ultimately you need to help him fall back to sleep on his own. Unfortunately, in order to correct this condition, some crying might take place. As taught in *Babywise*, when you respond to your baby's cry rationally, consider what is best for the baby in the long run. In this case, the continuance of excellent sleep patterns is best for the baby and his parents.

3. Our child is now standing in his crib but doesn't know how to get back down and begins to cry. What should we do?

Standing in the crib is half of a newly acquired skill. The other half is learning how to sit down after standing. You can aid the process by taking a few minutes after each nap to show him how to sit down. Take his hands firmly and guide them down the crib slats helping him sit. Over time he will get used to the sensation of letting himself down. If you go in every time to put him down, you're only delaying the learning process. There will be no need to learn to sit if he knows that when he cries Mom will always come to the rescue.

4. Our child keeps losing his pacifier at night and begins to cry. What should we do?

As stated previously, a sleep prop is any device needed to

help the child fall back to sleep once he awakens. In this case, the prop is the pacifier. It's probably time to wean him from it or you will become sleep deprived.

5. Our baby throws off his covers at night, gets cold, and then begins to cry. What do we do?

Children move around in their sleep, making it difficult to stay covered. As parents, you only have three preventative options. Dress your child warmly at night, turn up your central heating, or purchase a safe room heater. One caution to consider concerning nighttime sleep and room heaters is to be careful not to place your baby too close to a heater in hopes of compensating for the coldness of the night. It is a greater health threat for the child to become overheated than to be cold. Furthermore, heaters tend to dry the air, potentially causing respiratory problems with your baby. Please take note of this if you are using any type of portable heater.

6. My husband and I will be traveling for the next couple of weeks. How do we maintain the baby's routine, especially when we move through other time zones?

Here are a couple of suggestions. First, train your baby to sleep other places than in his crib. Second, learn how to adjust his routine to each new time zone. Let's start with the first challenge. When preparing for travel, a few weeks in advance put your child down for his naps or nighttime sleep in his playpen. For a couple of nights, put the playpen in the living room, family room, or your bedroom draping two sides with a couple of blankets. Take the blankets on your trip or borrow some when you arrive. The blankets serve to reduce potential distractions by closing in your child's sleep environment.

If your trip is within two time zones, time adjustments will be fairly automatic. When flying through three or four time zones, make adjustments to your baby's routine once you arrive. The type of adjustment depends on whether you are traveling east to west or west to east. With the first, you have an extended day; with the second, you have an early night. If you have an extended day, add another feeding and possibly a catnap. If you go west to east, split the bedtime difference in half between the old and new time zones.

For example, your baby's West Coast bedtime is 7:00 p.m. while the East Coast equivalent to 10:00 p.m. EST. Splitting the difference between the two zones will make your baby's first East Coast bedtime 8:30 p.m. Over the next couple of days, work his bedtime back to 7:00 p.m., making as many adjustments as needed to his daytime routine.

We suggest you limit sweet drinks and snacks while traveling. A trip is not the time to add extra sugar to your baby's diet, and extra snacks can suppress hunger to the point where it can affect digestive stabilization. Disrupting your baby's hunger metabolism often affects the sleep/wake cycles. Overall, your baby will be a joy to travel with, and the few problems you might encounter will be temporary.

7. My seven-month-old still fusses for five to ten minutes at each nap. Will he ever outgrow it, or am I doing something wrong?

Yes, your baby will outgrow it. Some babies tend to fuss more than others before settling into their nap, and this might continue up and through the next several months. Science cannot offer a complete explanation why some babies have a greater predisposition toward fussiness and seem to need a good cry once a day. As long as you know your baby is not hungry, sick, or in pain, and as long as he is taking good naps, that short period of fussing will eventually be a thing of the past.

8. My baby is sleeping 13 hours at night. Is this a problem?

Yes it is. The problem has a *cause* and a *effect*. The *cause* is usually (but not always) tied to poor or nonexistent daytime naps. In response, your baby is sleeping longer at night because of fatigue realized during the day. If naps are a problem, work on getting them established. As you do, his nighttime sleep will fall into a normal range.

The *effect* of extended nighttime sleep is the negative impact it has on a nursing mother's milk production. Do the math! Eleven hours is not a sufficient amount of time to replenish or maintain adequate nutrition through breastfeeding. If the extended sleep problem persist, contact your pediatrician.

SUMMARY

As your baby grows into the pretoddler stage, the amount of total sleep needed in a 24 hour period will gradually decline, although the quality of sleep will remain. This decline comes during the daytime as your baby's nap schedule transitions from three naps to two naps and then from two naps to one nap. Any problems you might encounter with your baby's sleep will be minor in comparison to the giant strides already made in his or her sleep stabilization.

Chapter Nine
The Topic Pool

W hile the most basic questions relating to a baby's feeding, waketime and naptime transitions were addressed in earlier chapters, there are always a few secondary, independent babyhood topics in need of comment or clarification. We arranged the topics below in alphabetical order for easy reference.

ACHIEVEMENT LEVELS

Much has been written about what a baby is supposed to be doing physically during the first year of his or her life. This includes mastering such things as shaking a rattle, saying "da-da", reaching for bright objects, crawling, and finally, walking. There are three important things to remember concerning your baby's level of achievement.

1. The daily routine you have your baby on enhances his ability to learn and process information. Repetition and predictability are key elements to the process of learning and a consistent routine provides these.

2. Babies differ in the age they master skills. If your sister's nine-month-old is starting to pull himself up to chairs and your nine-month old is still happily crawling, there is no cause for alarm. Avoid comparing your baby's development

to other babies. All children, by the time they start school will be walking, talking, feeding themselves and using the bathroom.

3. Along with your baby's physical development comes the corresponding mental capacities. Be careful not to focus solely on your baby's physical accomplishments. Talk to your baby! Young children can understand far more than they can verbalize.

BABY EQUIPMENT

The two most popular pieces of equipment for babies besides a playpen and stroller are the infant swing and infant walker.

The Infant Swing

A mechanical wind-up swing can serve two purposes. First, it can keep your baby peacefully occupied so Mom or Dad can get housework or other tasks done. Secondly, it helps soothe a fussy baby when nothing else works.

Infant swings have come a long way since we purchased our first one over forty years ago. Today, just about every conceivable option is available, including swings that play music as they rock. Two common features are multiple speeds when the swing rocks and a reclining option. Fussy babies tend to settle down better with the rocking motion at a stronger setting and speed. A slower speed is more conducive for relaxed, non-fussy times. The reclining option works well if you use the swing after feeding your baby, as this position takes pressure off his or her full tummy. Does your baby need all the fancy attachments? Probably not. Manufacturers tend to think in terms of what parents will buy more than what babies actually need.

There are some cautions to stay mindful of when using an infant swing. First, the AAP (American Academy of Pediatricians) recommends swings should not be used until your baby is capable of sitting up on his own. (This is usually achieved by seven to eight months of age.) However, most grandmothers will tell you that once your baby has good head and upper back control, the swing can be introduced in the reclining position as long as the baby is propped well and fully secured so he cannot move or slip out of the swing.

Second, swings should not be used for long periods of time. Fifteen to twenty minutes, twice a day is enough. The swing should never be out of the visual range of Mom or Dad. When using the swing to accomplish a task like preparing dinner, by all means, remember to talk to your baby while he or she is swinging.

Third, don't ever forget to keep the safety of your baby in mind when using equipment. Whether you purchase a new swing or borrow one from a friend or relative, make sure it is assembled well and has a wide base and a low center of gravity. While tipping a swing over is rare, it can happen if your baby leans too far over in one direction and the swing is not centered correctly. Another safety feature to look for includes a lap belt or shoulder harness. Never be in too much of a hurry when putting your baby in the swing to forget to secure the belt or harness.

Finally, we offer this word of caution. A swing is a tool parents can use, but it is not to be a substitute for human contact. Even if your baby is happy while in the swing, do not leave him there for long periods of time unsupervised. Neither should you let your baby sleep in the swing. The rocking motion does put babies to sleep, but that is not what the swing is for. When it is time for your baby to sleep, put him in his crib. That is not to say that you cannot use the swing to help your baby fall asleep when he is teething or over-stimulated and can't settle himself down, just don't let it become a habit.

The Baby Walker

The health risks of a baby walker far outweigh any benefit of allowing your baby to use one. With statistics showing walkers send more than 14,000 babies to the hospital every year, it is not difficult to understand why the AAP not only discourages the use of baby walkers, they have called for a ban on the manufacturing of them altogether. If you do choose to use a walker, please be extremely careful and under no circumstances should you let your baby out of your sight. Keep your baby away from stair-steps, wires and electric cords on the floor or within reach, and items with moving parts such as electric fans used in the summer months. For reasons of safety, we do not support the use of baby walkers for any reason.

BABY-PROOFING: YES OR NO?

Once your baby is able to crawl, stand, and move about, it will become necessary to provide boundaries by establishing what areas and items are off-limits to his exploring hands. Will your baby understand the "why" behind your instruction? Of course not. At this point in his development however, he does possess the capacity to understand what "No" or "Don't touch" means. When your baby is old enough to crawl, he can be taught to discriminate between what he can and cannot touch.

When deciding how to teach an active crawler what he can or cannot touch, parents need to decide if they are going to "baby-proof" their home or "home-proof" their baby. Which one is best for you and which one is best for your child?

Let's define the terms. "Baby-proofing" means that a child's unrestricted movements and momentary desires are necessary for his healthy development. Baby-proofing advocates claim (lacking scientific support) any restrictions or verbal restraints initiated by the parents towards their child regardless of the context of such limitations will negatively impact the child's ability to learn, become creative, and achieve a healthy self-esteem. Baby-proofing your home means you will rearrange your living area so your child is never placed in a situation where you would have to limit his freedom of exploration or confront him with the feared words, "No, don't touch."

"Home-proofing" your child means parents set appropriate limitations on their young child's mobility, introducing freedoms only when their child is old enough and wise enough to understand the concept of what "Don't touch" and "Be careful" means.

Prior to the 1970's, "home-proofing the child" was the common method of child-training used by society. The practice of "home-proofing" has a moral dimension to it as well. For example, when a child as young as eight-months-old learns he cannot touch the dog's eating dish, he is learning self-control and ultimately to obey. A huge value in "home-proofing" then, is that parents can start to teach their child the moral implications of obeying and other virtues at a very young age.

Capacity and Training

A five to twelve-month-old child is about to enter a transition that takes place over an extended period of time, taking him from the world of me, myself, and I (dominant in the first two years of life) to a world of understanding that other people and their property have equal significance. This is the world he will live in for the rest of his life. It seems reasonable then to *begin as you mean to go*.

Children nearing their first birthday have a growing awareness of the meaning of "boundaries". If faced with the temptation to play with Dad's fishing magazines lying on the coffee table or redirecting his little hands, redirecting can win out. How can you get your child to this point? Instead of rearranging your home ("baby-proofing"), you can train your child what is allowed and not allowed to be touched. Of course, there will be times when your child will strongly oppose your training efforts but you can over come those objections when you:

1. Stay consistent: If you are going to tell your child he can't touch something today then you must be prepared to tell him he can't touch that same item tomorrow, the next day and every day thereafter. Don't start what you don't mean to finish. In other words, if you aren't going to be consistent in your training efforts, by all means, "baby-proof" your home.

2. Understand correction will be necessary: Your child will touch the 'off-limits' item just to see if you mean business. You may try saying "No" again followed by a clap of your hands to get his attention. If he reaches out to touch it again, put your young child in his playpen for a few minutes to let him know you are serious. When he calms down, you may take him out of the playpen. If he goes back to the restricted item, back in the playpen he goes.

3. Take necessary precautions: If you have a valuable, breakable

or dangerous item and you do not want to take a chance it might get broken, remove it to a safe place. Secure the bookcase or wall-unit to the wall and place 'knick-knacks' and other fragile items out of reach. It is important that parents take every precaution to make their child's environment safe. Making your home safe for a young child is not the same thing as "baby-proofing" your home.

For your sake and to avoid frustrating your child, do not make his play area too big. If your son or daughter develops a fondness with the toilet seat in the bathroom, shut the door and keep it closed. How is this different from "baby-proofing"? With "baby-proofing", everything a child can touch is removed. When you create a play environment that has limitations for the child, there are still many items in the home he cannot touch. Again, please do not underestimate the moral implications of "home-proofing" your child.

NURSERIES AND BABY-SITTERS

Parents should be appreciative when leaving a child in a nursery, day-care or with a baby-sitter. Nursery or day-care workers cannot be expected to maintain your baby's routine because there is no way they can keep track of the different routines of each child in their care. Leave a bottle of water, formula, or breastmilk and give the attendant the freedom to do what she thinks is best for your baby and the others in the nursery.

When you have a well established routine, a couple of hours in a nursery setting will not throw your child off. When you and baby get home, make the appropriate adjustments. This is the beauty of having an established schedule. It allows for flexibility during the times most needed, but the existing patterns of order and routine are quickly reestablished when needed.

Baby-sitters who come into your home can follow your routine closer than the nursery worker because she or he is there to specifically care for your child. The wise thing to do is leave a written schedule of activities. This will take much of the guess work out for the sitter and provide specific instructions.

DENTAL CARE AND YOUR BABY

Your child should see a dentist around the time his first tooth comes into his mouth, which usually occurs around six months of age. At the very least, make sure your child sees a dentist for a "well-baby dental check-up" by his first birthday. This is very important because early evaluation and education are the keys to the prevention of dental diseases. Your dentist can help you determine your child's risk for decay and help you with techniques to clean his teeth effectively and safely. In addition to having your child evaluated, starting to visit the dentist at an early age will help your child become comfortable in a dental office.

Severe early childhood decay can be devastating to the child and even more so for the parents as their child goes through extensive dental procedures. In some cases, the disease can be so advanced that by the time the child is evaluated he will require general anesthesia to safely complete the needed treatments. Prevention is the way to go!

Cleaning and Preventing Decay

Begin cleaning your baby's teeth when the first tooth comes into the mouth. All that is needed to clean your baby's teeth is a wet washcloth, which is gently rubbed against the teeth. You can also use a child-sized toothbrush. Toothpaste is not necessary at this early age. Ideally, cleaning your baby's teeth should be done at least twice a day with special attention at night just before bedtime.

Do not let your baby go to bed with a bottle or a non-spill sippy cup that contains anything other than water. The AAPD (American Academy of Pediatric Dentists) recommends that when juice is offered, it should be in a cup and children should be weaned from the bottle between the ages of twelve and fourteen months. Infants and toddlers who suffer from decay are more likely to continue to have similar problems when they get their permanent teeth. Therefore, starting habits early like good teeth cleanings, limiting juice and sugary snacks, and regular visits to the dentist are keys to unlock life-long oral health in your child.

Teething and Sickness

When a tooth begins to break through the gum, this is referred to as "teething". Teething is not a disease, but a part of normal growth. Teething should not interfere with breastfeeding since the sucking reflex used while nursing is done by the tongue and palate, not the gums. Discomfort, irritability, fussiness, increased salivation, and a slightly raised temperature can accompany the eruption of a tooth. As uncomfortable as a child might appear, parents should not regard teething as a catch-all excuse for chronic poor behavior or a drastic change in their baby's routine.

Teething can disrupt your baby's sleep. How can you comfort your baby without losing his good sleep habits? First, understand that the process of cutting teeth does not disrupt sleep for all babies. While there is some discomfort, it may not be enough to override your baby's well-established sleep patterns. Second, realize this discomfort is temporary. Babies do not cut teeth for weeks. For most babies it takes place over a couple of days. You can get over-the-counter teething gels at a drugstore that serve to numb the gum enough to allow a baby to relax and go back to sleep.

If the problem is so serious it keeps your baby awake, comfort him in a rocking chair but do not take him to bed with you or feed him. Even one night in bed with his parents will give a baby the idea this is a much nicer place to be than alone in his crib! Comfort when comfort is needed, but when those teeth finally break through, get back to your baby's regular routine as quickly as possible. Babies can continue to waken during the night when the teething episode has passed. They need to relearn how to fall back to sleep on their own.

Illnesses can be handled in a similar manner. Keep your baby as close to his routine as possible when he is sick and follow your doctor's advice regarding the use of medicine. Usually a decrease in appetite will accompany an illness. Do not force your child to eat, but make sure to maintain adequate liquid intake as prescribed by your pediatrician. Again, provide comfort when comfort is needed, but avoid habit-forming practices that will need correction in the future.

After an illness passes, it may take up to three days before a baby goes back to his regular routine. So, once your baby returns to health, get him back to his nap and nighttime sleep routine without delay.

IMMUNIZATIONS

The ability to protect our children from the tragedies of polio and other deadly diseases is one of the blessings of our day. Medical research has provided us with effective immunizations that build up antibodies to fight off invading disease. But the vaccines are useless if a child never receives them. Parents are responsible to see that their child is fully protected. The eight common vaccinations offered are polio, diphtheria, pertussis (whooping cough), tetanus, rubella (German measles), mumps, measles, hepatitis, and Haemophilus influenza, type B (Hib). Most pediatricians start routine immunizations within the first two months after a baby is born.

Because immunization schedules change frequently as better vaccines and updated information is available, you will need to check with your pediatrician for a recent time-table of vaccinations. Most importantly, stay current with making sure your baby is receiving his on schedule. If you have concerns or questions about any vaccine, contact your pediatrician. He or she will be a more reliable source than internet chat rooms discussing the pros and cons of vaccinations.

THE MICROWAVE AND THE BOTTLE

Occasionally you may want to heat your baby's bottle in a microwave oven. This can be dangerous unless caution is used. Microwaves heat foods unevenly, so be sure to shake the bottle well after heating and squirt a dab of milk on your wrist to test for warmth. When heating your baby's bottle, loosen the top to allow for heat expansion, otherwise it may explode.

Unlike formula, breastmilk should not be heated in microwaves. The heat inside a microwave is so intense it will destroy the benefits contained in breastmilk. Heat breast-milk by putting it into a pan of warm water. This is the best way to ensure that the milk is not overheated and that necessary nutrients are not destroyed.

SLEEP AND LEARNING

Last night was a rough one. The dog was barking and the

electricity went out due to a thunderstorm, causing the alarm clock by your bed to flash when the power came back on. Throughout the ordeal, you never got out of bed. You don't recall being awake, although you figured out something had happened when your alarm didn't go off. It does not take long for you to realize something happened other than your alarm going haywire—you are cranky, edgy, and just not nice to be around. Simply put, you got a lousy night's sleep and every raw nerve-ending in your body stands ready to let everyone you meet know this.

When it comes to children, parents tend only to think in terms of these two things: either their child is asleep or he is awake. There is a blending scale of sleep and wake-times. Sleep ranges from a completely relaxed state to active sleep, to groggy wake-time to complete wakefulness. Optimal wakefulness is directly tied to optimal sleep, and optimal development is directly tied to optimal wakefulness. We cannot overemphasize this point. Children who suffer from a lack of healthy naps and nighttime sleep also experience a type of passive chronic fatigue, effecting maximum alertness.

The effect of too little sleep is equally devastating, affecting a child's alertness as well. When a child is not alert, his inattentiveness is increased while his ability to focus and concentrate is decreased. This child is easily distracted and often physically hyperactive. He is also more demanding, and cannot interact within a learning environment for sustained periods of time.

In contrast, children who have established healthy sleep habits are optimally awake and optimally alert to interact with their environment. Having observed a generation of these children now, we see common threads when they get to school-age. In classroom settings, these children are more self-assured, happier, less demanding, more sociable, creative and motivated. They have longer attention spans and become faster learners because they are more adaptable. Mediocrity among these children is rare, while excellence is common.

In *Babywise,* we spoke about a child's ability to learn. We noted that while parents cannot alter a child's intelligence quotient, they can maximize or limit it. One way this is done, both positively and negatively, is through sleep. The impact healthy and not-so-healthy sleep has on educational outcomes was first noted in a 1925 study conducted by Dr. Lewis M. Terman. Amazingly, his insights and conclusions related to factors influencing I.Q. continue to stand unchallenged to this day. His study looked at over two-thousand children with superior intelligence and found one common line—all of them had experienced consistent healthy nighttime sleep. Good sleep habits are not a child's choice, but a parental decision.

THE WALKING MILESTONE

A pretoddler's mobility is nothing new. He began by creeping, then crawling, standing, and then moving from object to object. Then, one day it happened—he took that first step. From that point forward, his world began to change and so did yours. Walking is a developmental milestone because it marks a new era of toddler independence. Now his little feet can take him where his mind desires. If he is on the go, you will not be far behind.

Walking also ushers in a new era of parental supervision because it increases a child's contacts. Mobility opens doors of opportunity and new areas of interest, exploration, and adventure, which require constant parental supervision. Now your baby is also able to walk to mischief and trouble. As a crawler you knew his range of exploration. As a walker, you now must keep your eye on him since his ability and resolve to get from here to there far exceeds his judgment of caution and safety.

During the one year span between twelve and twenty-four months, the walking, talking, exploring pretoddler multiplies the demands of mother's time, energy, and patience more than any other period of his life. It is also a time when clashes of the "will" abound, for the walking-about pretoddler is in the process of not only testing his legs but also trying new experiences with his hands. His mind has caught up with his legs, so asserting himself accompanies his mobility. If left to himself unhindered by moral and safety concerns, this little person could empty a book shelf in minutes, connect with Hong Kong on Dad's cell phone, drink from the bird-bath, splash little hands in the toilet, drain the last sips of the beverage left on the coffee table, flee the kitchen with a table knife, or take a nap in the dog house — which, after everything else, would be a positive thing.

Ah yes, the mobile pretoddler. There is no question that a pretoddler's mom is a tired mom, and for good reason. The emotional and physical energy needed to supervise an energy-packed tot can take down the most physically fit mom. If your child happens to be a boy, add fifty percent more energy. Never so beautiful does this child look to his weary mom as he does when he closes his eyes in sleep.

Why bring up the topic of walking at this point? Because some babies begin walking at nine months while others at eighteen months of age. Regardless of when this milestone is reached, the feeding, waketime, and naptime foundations outlined in this book will greatly impact your ability to manage your soon to be mobile child.

BOOK SUMMARY

There is no greater fulfillment a parent can receive than the upturned face of a child, eyes speaking wonders and a face of confidence in discovering a brand new world with Mom and Dad. While there is still work to be done in the remaining pre-toddler months, rest assured, the foundations laid during the five to twelve month period of time (with his feeding/waketime/naptime successes) will pay huge dividends in the next phase of growth and development. *Begin as you mean to go* and continue in that way. Enjoy your pretoddler.

Section Two Summary Points

Highchair Challenges

1. Direct and redirect baby's behavior with your voice tone.
2. Utilize an attention getting hand squeeze.
3. Teach your baby consequences by removing items he should not be touching.
4. Removing the child isolates him from the problem.
5. Remember — training and correction is a process.
6. Physical correction is not an age-appropriate form of correction for babies and pretoddlers.

Waketime & Creative Learning Activities

1. Playpen Benefits:
   a. It offers a structured learning environment.
   b. It promotes and reinforces the development of longer attention span.
   c. It provides a safe environment.
   d. It encourages self-play adeptness rather than your baby becoming dependent on being entertained.
2. Start with short increments of time and gradually increase playpen-time.
3. Playpen Basics:
   a. Use at approximately the same time each day.
   b. Use the playpen when your child is alert.
   c. Do not clutter with too many toys.
   d. Keep toys age-appropriate.
   e. Keep playpen-time age-appropriate.
4. "Playpen-time" will transition to "Roomtime" around 18 months of age.

Naps and Nighttime Sleep

1. "Wake-up Happy" Rules:
   a. Mom decides when the nap begins.
   b. Mom decides when the nap ends.
   c. More sleep is need if baby wakes up cranky.
2. Evaluating disturbed naptime periods:
   a. Investigate the immediate situation.
   b. Babies will wake up hungry during growth spurts.
   c. Sometimes restless babies just need to cuddle.
   b. Become a student of your child's sleep and wake temp-erament. Every child is different.

Common Sleep Questions

1. Always consider the possibility that your baby is hungry.
2. Your baby might need more nutrition that comes from solid food.
3. It might be time to drop an afternoon nap.
4. A drastic change in your baby's routine will affect his sleep.
5. If your child can stand in his crib, he can learn how to get down.
6. Start to remove your baby's pacifier at naptimes before taking it away at nighttime.
7. Dress your baby for cooler nights in case he loses his blankets during sleep.
8. Train your baby to sleep in other places than his crib and adjust his routine when moving into a new time zone. This will make traveling easier.
9. Good naps help alleviate extended fussy times.

Section Two — Questions For Review

1. Please name and briefly describe the four methods of corrective discipline for pretoddlers.
   a.

   b.

   c.

   d.

2. What educational benefit does the playpen serve?

3. At what age could you extend your pretoddler's playpentime to thirty minutes?

4. What are the three "Wake-up Happy" rules?
   a.

   b.

   c.

5. List some reasons why pretoddlers might wake-up early.

6. Explain the difference between a tired baby and a fatigued baby?

Appendix A
Child Language Development

꧁꧂

Anyone attempting to learn a language can tell you that it can be a very difficult task, and it takes years to achieve any sort of fluency. God has equipped babies with a phenomenal ability to achieve total fluency in about three years, with very little practice and almost no conscious thought required. Parents are the models God has provided for a child's development, and the area of language development is no different from the many others discussed in this guide.

In your infant's world, there are only sounds, no words. The more you talk to your baby the stronger the formation of a dedicated connection in the brain's auditory cortex. The more words your baby hears *from you*, the faster he develops his language skills. Here are some ideas to help you help your child develop language.

1. It is not necessary to use "baby talk." It is very tempting to reduce what you are saying to what you think the baby understands, such as "Ryan, no touch, that bad." Children are wonderful decoders. If you say, "Ryan, don't touch that, it's bad," he will (even at the young age of six months) understand the tone of voice, the facial expression, and any gestures you might use. By twelve to fourteen months, he'll understand enough of the words and intonations to figure out exactly what you are telling him. Children are wonderful imitators, too. Why not

give them a chance to learn the correct sentence structure by speaking it yourself?

2. Talk about anything and everything! This gives your child a chance to pair words with concepts. Even though he will not understand all the words at first, what a great exposure to the world you are giving him. When you go to the grocery store, talk about what you are getting, where you are going next, things you see in the aisles. A pretoddler certainly doesn't understand everything, but you are laying a broad foundation for the future.

3. Read, read, read! Reading books to your child is a wonderful way to expose him to words and concepts. (We recommend Jim Trelease's Read-Aloud Handbook, Penguin Books: N.Y., N.Y.) which helps children become aid readers

4. Once your child starts speaking, expand on what he says. For example, you are giving your son a bath, and he says, "Boat down." You could respond by saying, "Yes, the boat went down." This not only recognizes what your child has said, but also gives him the correct form of a full sentence. Cute though it is, you really do not want your child to start kindergarten using baby sentences!

5. Above all, relax! With few exceptions, children learn language in spite of anything parents do or think they have done to inhibit it!

CHILD LANGUAGE DEVELOPMENT
The following is a general outline of the stages of child language

development. Each child develops at his own rate, and the ages given are approximate.

Birth to 3 months: A familiar, friendly voice comforts him. He smiles at Mom or another familiar person. He has different cries for hunger, dirty diaper, and fatigue. He coos and goos.

2 to 4 months: He pays attention to the person speaking to him, responds to an angry tone of voice by crying, and turns toward a source of sound. He laughs out loud and begins to babble making sounds like "bababa."

4 to 6 months: He begins to respond to his environment and begins to understand inflection and intensity of utterances. He strings several different sounds together "badaba-daba," and he blows raspberries.

6 to 9 months: He listens with greater attention to others' utterances, understands words such as "no", "bye-bye", and his name. He begins to echo sounds and actions that others make.

9 to 12 months: He begins following simple directions ("Do not touch", "Come here") and shakes his head yes and no. The long-awaited first word appears and he begins to "jargon" (strings of sounds paired with intonations to sound like questions, statements, or demands).

12 to 18 months: He recognizes familiar objects and people and identifies body parts. He adds more and more words and begins to put short sentences together.

<u>18 to 24 months</u>: He identifies more and more objects when requested to do so and listens to simple stories.

The ages listed above are only a guide and indicate when most children exhibit the language skill listed. Don't worry if your child is a month or two late at attaining any given level for children mature at different rates. If your child is not responding to you by the age of one year, or not speaking at all by the age of two years, you should seek referrals to the appropriate professionals from your child's doctor.

Finally, just as a reminder, early video watching for children under the age of two will have a negative affect on speech development. This is one reason the American Academy of Pediatrics does not endorse screen images for infants. Your baby's brain has circuits in the auditory cortex representing sounds that form words. They become hard wired by the age of one year. Research strongly suggest the more words a child hears by the age of two years, the larger his vocabulary. However, the method by which words are transferred is as important as the words themselves. During these early ages, nothing beats the human factor and the two-way communication that comes from Mom and Dad's voice. This is something videos cannot do!

Appendix B
What Makes Your Baby a Person

Nature has a keen way of tutoring parents. Observe the gardener with his plants. He does not create the bloom, or the petal, or the stem that produces the petal. He cannot grow the plant or make it more beautiful. He is neither its creator nor its architect. The power of life and beauty lies within the plant itself. The gardener however, knows the environment. He knows the right amount of sunshine and moisture required for the unfolding of every blossom. He knows the time of pruning, training, and fertilizing that is necessary to bring the plant to a beautiful bloom. Yet the gardener is neither the life of the plant nor the source, but he is the nurturer of the life placed before him.

Picture your baby's life unfolding like a beautiful bloom. You, the parent, serve as the bloom's keeper. No other influence can affect the life of your child quite like you—a loving, caring parent. You are more than a nurturer of nature; you are the guardian. You matter greatly in the life-formation of your child. This leads us to observe the real work of parents as loving mentors.

We know that your emerging pretoddler has his own peculiar way. He will think in the here and now, with no tomorrow in sight. He is not easily moved to self-restraint or seeks to secure some future blessings. "A penny saved is a penny earned" is quite beyond his grasp and interest. And all his nursery peers would agree that crying over spilled milk is essential if you're really thirsty—you'll get more milk faster that way!

As your pretoddler transitions into the early stages of toddlerhood, he will first be concerned with the concrete, not the abstract. Moral qualities such as justice, mercy, and truth are quite beyond his reach, but he does understand these qualities when expressed toward him. His actions and developing speech reflect his self-oriented desires rather than socialized values that will change in a few years.

Clearly the adult life, while distinct from childhood and adolescence, is wholly built upon the foundation of early training parents put into their children. It is important to see that a child is adequately prepared from the beginning for a safe arrival in the many stations of life, starting with understanding all the components that make up the little soon-to-be crawling person emerging under your roof.

What goes into making your baby a person? Apart from the spiritual elements reflecting the Creator's thumbprint on your baby's soul, there are a variety of biological influences, including things you cannot control, i.e. nature, heredity, temperament, and predispositions, and those influences shaped by your beliefs including nurture, environment, education, values, and goals.

There is also the natural order of growth and development of children bringing new and changing variables into play. As the baby's body grows, so grows his mind, and so grows his interplay with the rest of humanity. These factors combined make up the human quality of our being.

To prepare your thinking for what awaits you just around the developmental corner, consider the influence of *heredity*, *environment* and the factors shaping your child's *personality*.

Your Baby's Life is Controlled by HEP

Little Joey swings a stick and suddenly he's slated for College All-Stars twenty years down the road. Abby twists a silk scarf around her neck and she's destined to be a fashion designer following her momma's footsteps. Far-fetched? Not exactly. We are all influenced by the forces of heredity, environment, and personality. Nineteenth century Dartmouth College professor, H. H. Horne in his book *Idealism in Education*, links these relationships in plain words:

1. Heredity bestows capacity
2. Environment provides opportunity
3. Personality recognizes capacity and improves opportunity

Each of these forces combine together to shape all of us—you, me, and your sweetheart napping in the next room. The same Professor Horne is credited with saying, "A child is born in part, he is made in part, and in part he makes himself." We believe that is an accurate assessment of life. Heredity, it has been said, determines what your child can do, and environment determines what your child will do. Supervising all three aspects are the caretakers of life—enter stage right, Mom and Dad.

Heredity

After conception, nothing can be done to add to or subtract from our hereditary endowment. If Grandpa's left ear turns out along the back edge, just like your mother's left ear which looks amazingly like your own, guess what? Don't be surprised if one or more of your own beautiful blooms sports the telltale "Grandpa ear". Other traits, while not visible to the eye, are doled out with equal clarity. Is there a trait in your pretoddler that you do not like? Take a look at the family photos hanging in the hallway. Do you see the relative that's smirking? He's probably the one to blame.

A child inherits one-half of his genetic self from his two parents, one fourth of his characteristics from the four grand-parents, and one-eighth of his biological distinctiveness from eight great-grandparents. Heredity passes to each generation two categories of traits — fixed and fluid. Fixed genetic traits are immune to nurturing influences. Fluid tendencies however, are greatly impacted by the nurturing process.

For example, outward distinctions such as red hair, green eyes, short arms, big ears, cute nose, and dimpled chins are fixed endowments. They are what they are, straight from the genetic cabbage patch. Have you ever wondered where that nose came from? Nothing in genetic sight among the parents? "Your baby got that from Uncle Fabio, on your mother's side," says Aunt Regina. A hidden surprise from the family tree.

Heredity also passes fluid endowments. These are propensi-ties, tendencies, and capacities. Intelligence potential, aptitudes and special levels of giftedness are all fluid, meaning this side of the hereditary equation is markedly influenced by the nurturing environment. That is why heredity determines what a child can do, and the environment determines what a child will do.

We have friends endowed with the gift and talent for music. Mom and Dad each play a combination of instruments includ-ing harp, piano, trumpet, guitar, flute, trombone, French horn, and the oboe. What did their children inherited? It was not their parent's knowledge of music, but an ear, aptitude, capacity and interest in music. Natural propensities spawned in the right environment produced, in this case, multi-talented musical children. But the genetic endowment was nurtured. Without the nurturing environment, the beautiful seeds of endowment, like the frozen pods in the tundra, lie dormant until the conditions are right to bloom. Unfortunately, human environments are less predictable than seasonal ones.

What does this mean for you and your baby? If the nurturing environment is to stimulate genetic potentials and maximize those potentials, it needs three things from Mom and Dad.

First, you need awareness. In the Ezzo family line, Gary's father was a talented musician. He played a number of string instruments and the piano with pep. Of three sons, only one inherited the father's musical talent. Gary was not the one. In the next generation when Gary and his wife Anne Marie were raising their children, they knew there was a possibility for some musical giftedness. But possibility does not equate to certainty, and it was soon realized that no great musical genetic endowment fell on their offspring.

The point here is that of awareness. The Ezzos knew of a genetic propensity for musical ability. Because of it, they created a nurturing environment to determine if any gene slipped through the family line, and then responded to the opportunity by introducing formalized music lessons in their children's primary years.

What is in your family tree? Go back two generations, to parents and grandparents, and write up a list of endowment possibilities. Talk to relatives, great-aunts and uncles, and older cousins. Was Grandpa highly inventive? Was Mom an artisan of quilts? Was there an uncle gifted in mathematics, or a sister endowed with a massive vocabulary and a creative mind? Become aware of the genetic endowments of your recent family lineage. Maybe you'll find a squirrel in your family tree which will finally account for Billy's need to store up every scrap of paper, every piece of ribbon, and every pebble he ever touched.

Second, you can maximize your baby's genetic potential when you parent the "whole child" rather than just a single trait. Hurray for you if your child is a budding Rembrandt, Mozart, Galileo or Edison, but can he entertain himself when playing by himself? Can he get along with other children? Can your little star kick a ball and gently spend time with baby sister? Don't err like Schroeder's mom did. Schroeder is the Peanuts character that spent his entire cartoon life hunched over a piano composing music.

While any unfavorable parent attitude can result in unhealthy outcomes, that which has the most damaging and far-reaching effect is the concept of the dream child. Parents create a genetic ideal and force the child into a very narrow category of interest. As a result, the emotional pressure to attain dream child status, mixed with the lack of normal childhood experiences hinders genetic potential if not wounding it.

Third, no wonderful gift of hereditary endowment can be matured if not surrounded by the basic disciplines of life. Writing the latest, greatest American novel will be impossible if your would-be author never develops the focus needed for reading. Piano practice becomes a battle if your child never learned to sit and concentrate. Yes, there's that playpen thing again. Sitting, focusing concentrating.

We hope we made our point. A child cannot learn until he is ready to learn. He cannot achieve until the biological clock says it's time. He cannot master any skill without the accompanying resources of self-control and self-governance. This means that regardless of what giftedness or talent your child possesses, or what wonderful genetic endowment he may have inherited, it needs to be nurtured in the total context of childhood and childhood training. If it is not, that giftedness, while possibly discovered, will eventually reach a plateau in learning and show little improvement from that time forward. Remember the gardener analogy? Good seeds planted in poor soil will result in stunted plants. So it is with our children. That leads to some thoughts regarding the learning environment your baby is growing in.

Environment

With both heredity and environment, children are recipients. Regarding the environment, the home has dominant control. Mom and Dad provide the environment for the most impressionable years of life. The difficulty, if not the downfall of laissez-faire parenting is not realizing how education shapes the habits of the heart, and in so doing, weds genetic propensities with right stimulation. The positive forces of heredity do not always find a healthy and nourishing environment. When good capacity is denied the right environment, the legacy is at best less than a child's full potential, and at worst, a generational disaster. What can a parent glean from this fact? One supreme thought: The beliefs that drive your parenting can and will affect generations to come. That is another way of reminding you to *begin as you mean to go.*

Personality

Energetic Noah does everything big. He'll march into a

room, all smiles, and give Grandma a great big hug. Hopping to the room's center, he delights his eager audience with an impromptu performance. Finally, in grand finale, he drops to the floor to roll himself out the door. When Mom calls him to sit beside her, he cries, and staying true to the end, his distress and resistance is huge. Is his high-flying, crash-and-burn style a sign of a testy temperament, or are we now in the personality zone? What's the difference anyway?

Let's take a look. Few words used in contemporary theory of child development are as ambiguous as the term "personality". The term suggests a variety of meanings to different theorist. We have all heard the expression, "he's a chip off the old block," implying that personality is inherited and not subject to change. Not so on either account.

We provide a very simple definition for the sake of continuity. Personality is a composite of three variables: heredity, environment, and temperament. Temperament (inborn into human personality) speaks to the general categories of uniqueness, which greatly influence a child's perceptions and reactions. You can distinguish between a child's temperament and his personality by saying that temperament traits are inborn while personality traits are the result of nature and nurture. Heredity is what your genetic history brings to personality, environment is what the home and society add, and temperament is the child's contribution.

If that sounds confusing then take relief with this bit of news. Your child's personality is the last thing you need to worry about. That's because personality is the sum of each influence shaping the formation of our being. It is not one definite, specific attribute; rather it is the quality of the individual's total behavior. You cannot change the whole without changing the parts, and some parts cannot be changed.

For example, you cannot change your child's temperament anymore than a leopard can change its spots. You can understand it and cooperate with it, but not alter it. You cannot alter the hereditary influences on your children, but you can minimize the negative propensities, strengthen areas of weakness, encourage areas of strength, and maximize areas of giftedness.

The only area you have enormous influence over in the formation of personality is in creating the right educational environment for your baby. Education impacts personality. The learning environment fostered will make all the difference in the world for your baby and soon to be toddler.

When we speak of education we do so in the broadest sense. This goes way beyond textbook learning. Learning and schooling are not synonymous, but both are vehicles of education. Most of your parenting will be devoted to educating your children in three vital areas of life until they achieve mastery themselves: morality, health and safety, and life skills.

Your child's personality is greatly shaped by your educational fervency. For example, in the toddler years you will begin to teach how to be kind, good, caring, patient, generous, and responsible. You will also help him form healthy habits—how to brush his teeth, take a bath, and manage his personal care. Accenting these educational goals is more education, such as teaching the child how to think, how to make sound judgments, and apply logic and reason to his life.

The next major phase of your baby's development expands on all factors of learning that place you, mom and dad in the driver's seat. The good news is how far you have come already. Before you know it, the *babyhood transition* phase will soon be a thing of the past but the foundations you laid with feeding, waketime activities and healthy sleep habits will travel with your baby into the next major milestone of life: the walking, talking, exploring mobile toddler. Happy parenting.

Subject Index

More Resources
by Gary Ezzo and Dr. Robert Bucknam

With over two million homes to their credit, trusted parenting authors Gary Ezzo and Dr. Robert Bucknam bring their collective wisdom, experience, and insights to bear on these critical phases of growth and development.

On Becoming Babywise
On Becoming Babywise gained national and international recognition for its immensely sensible approach to nurturing a newborn. The infant management plan offered by Ezzo and Bucknam successfully and naturally helps infants synchronize their feeding/waketime and nighttime sleep cycles. The results? You have a happy, healthy and contented baby who will begin sleeping through the night on average between seven and nine weeks of age.

On Becoming Babywise II
This series teaches the practical side of introducing solid foods, managing mealtimes, nap transitions, traveling with your infant, setting reasonable limits while encouraging healthy exploration and much more. You will learn how to teach your child to use sign language for basic needs, a tool proven to help stimulate cognitive growth and advance communication.

On Becoming Pretoddlerwise
The period between twelve and eighteen months places a child on a one-way bridge to the future. Infancy is a thing of the past and toddlerhood is straight ahead. A baby still? Not really, but neither is he a toddler and that is the key to understanding this phase of growth. This is a period of metamorphosis when his potential for learning seems limitless, his budding curiosity unquenchable and his energy level never seems to diminish. It is also a period of great

exchange: baby food is exchanged for table food; the highchair for booster seat; finger feeding is replaced with spoon; babbling sounds will transition to speaking, the first unsteady steps are conquered by strides of confidence, and the list goes on. *On Becoming Pretoddlerwise* will help any parent acquire useful knowledge that will prepare them for what lies around the next corner – the reality of toddlerhood where change sometimes comes every day.

On Becoming Toddlerwise

The toddler years are learning fields and you need a trustworthy guide to take you through the unfolding maze of your child's developing world. *On Becoming Toddlerwise* is a toolchest of workable strategies and ideas that multiply your child's learning opportunities in a loving and nurturing way. This resource is as practical as it is informative.

On Becoming Pottywise for Toddlers

Potty training doesn't have to be complicated and neither should a resource that explains it. *On Becoming Pottywise for Toddlers* looks to developmental readiness cues of children as the starting point of potty training. While no promise can be made, we can tell you that many moms successfully complete their training in a day or two, some achieve it literally in hours.

On Becoming Preschoolwise

Gary Ezzo and Dr. Robert Bucknam once again bring their collective wisdom, experience, and insight to bear on this critical phase of preschool training. From teaching about the importance of play to learning how to prepare a preschooler for the first day of school, from organizing your child's week to understanding childhood fears and calming parental anxiety; sound advice and practical application await the reader.

On Becoming Childwise

Equip yourself with fifteen practical principles for training kids in the art of living happily amongst family and friends. Foster the safe, secure growth of your child's self-concept and worldview. *On Becoming Childwise* shows you how to raise emotionally balanced, intellectually assertive and morally sensible children. It's the essential guidebook for the adventurous years from toddler to grade-schooler!

On Becoming Preteenwise

The middle years, eight to twelve years of age, are perhaps the most significant attitude-forming period in the life of a child. It is during this time that the roots of moral character are established. From the foundation that is formed, healthy or not-so-healthy family relationships will be built. These are the years when patterns of behavior are firmly established – patterns that will impact your parent-child relationship for decades to come. Rightly meeting the small challenges of the middle years significantly reduces the likelihood of big challenges in the teen years.

On Becoming Teenwise

Why do teenagers rebel? Is it due to hormones, a suppressed primal desire to stake out their own domain, or a natural and predictable process of growth? To what extent do parents encourage or discourage the storm and stress of adolescence? *On Becoming Teenwise* looks at the many factors that make living with a teenager a blessing or a curse. It exposes the notions of secular myth and brings to light the proven how-to applications of building and maintaining healthy relationships with your teens. Whether you worry about your teen and dating or your teen and drugs, the principles of *On Becoming Teenwise* are appropriate and applicable for both extremes and everyone in-between. They do work!